EMPOWERING THE CHURCH

WITNESS

EMPOWERING THE CHURCH
Through Worship, Community, and Mission

A. GRACE WENGER
DAVE & NETA JACKSON

HERALD PRESS
Scottdale, Pennsylvania
Kitchener, Ontario

Library of Congress Cataloging-in-Publication Data
Wenger, A. Grace, 1919-
    Witness : empowering the church through worship, community, and
mission / A. Grace Wenger and Dave and Neta Jackson.
       p.   cm.
    Rev. ed. of: God builds the church through congregational witness.
1963, c1962.
    Bibliography: p.
    ISBN 0-8361-3482-6 (pbk.)
    1. Witness bearing (Christianity)   2. Evangelistic work.
I. Jackson, Dave.   II. Jackson, Neta.   III. Wenger, A. Grace, 1919-
God builds the church through congregational witness.   IV. Title.
BV4520.W4 1989
269'.2—dc19   88-24492
                                                             CIP

The paper used in this publication meets the minimum requirements of
American National Standard for Information Sciences—Permanence of
Paper for Printed Library Materials, ANSI Z39.48-1984.

Scripture quotations, unless otherwise noted, are from the *Holy Bible: New
International Version.* Copyright © 1973, 1978 1984, by the International Bible Society. Used by permission of Zondervan Bible Publishers.

The sign on the front cover is the symbol of faith, the patient expectation of
salvation coming from above.

Contents

Foreword

Many congregations today are searching for ways to effectively reach out to the unchurched but remain motionless and stymied. They have members who love the Lord, are loyal to the congregation, and who work hard within the church. But the church doesn't seem to be going anywhere. It seems to be more engaged in setting up events at the church for Christians to attend rather than establishing a strategy for reaching the unchurched. What needs to happen, then, to transform this mind-set and reform this kind of congregation?

A study of this book may set the stage for renewed thinking about what the local church is all about. Dave and Neta Jackson tackle this subject in a thought-provoking and knowledgeable way.

This book, based on an earlier work by A. Grace Wenger entitled *God Builds the Church Through Congregational Witness*, takes the basic concepts set forth by Wenger and helps the reader apply them to the church today. New illustrations of personal and congregational witness based on biblical principles tell the reader, "This might work for you, too!" Examples retained from the original book show that methods and techniques do not always need innovation. Yet the authors make it clear that we need to keep up-to-date as a witness to our everchanging communities.

The progression of this book is striking. The Jacksons take

Wenger's basic outline, inserting a chapter here and there that speaks to issues that congregations need to consider in the great commission business as they face the twenty-first century. They integrate personal witness within congregational outreach. These need to be two sides of the same coin. Otherwise, persons brought to faith through individual witness will soon die if they are not gathered within the loving care of fellow Christians.

Congregations to be evangelistic do not have to revitalize their church structure, set up more committees, or even recruit every last member to get involved. Through vivid examples, the Jacksons show that witness can emerge out of groups already in existence in the church as long as there is some intentionality for outreach and verbal witness that gets worked into the system. Worship services, where members show to newcomers that they believe God is real, are in themselves a witness. There is also a witness in bringing the unchurched within the fellowship of believers where they see love and understanding even in difficult circumstances. The chapter which speaks of family-to-family evangelism is rich with challenges and ideas.

One of the added strengths of this book is the format of 13 chapters, which can be used for a congregational study over a three-month period. The soundness of the principles set forth and the encouragement of the examples given will engender much discussion in a Sunday school class or a small group. Its applicability is certain if the local congregation which studies this book really desires to be effective. The authors haven't missed much in scriptural foundation and practical application that, if followed, could turn your church around. Individuals who study on their own will be given new ideas to apply to congregational goal-setting and strategy.

We need this book today. It combines sound theory with useful practicality. Local churches will want to digest and use these concepts and ideas to seek and serve those who are still outside the loving care of the congregation.

—G. Edwin Bontrager
Congregational Outreach Director
Mennonite Board of Missions

Witness:
The Purpose of
the Church

The church is called to be a corporate witness and through the Holy Spirit to empower all its members in witnessing. The good news to be shared is that God desires, through Christ, to receive all people into his family, the church. Christ commissions his followers to be his witnesses, touching others with forgiveness and life in Christ.

CHAPTER ONE

Witnessing Together

The idea was to deliver a *Doorstep Evangel* to every home in our part of the city. Somewhere along the way we were bound to run into people who were hungry for the Lord.

I knocked on dozens of doors and did find a few people in pretty deep need. But, I don't know, it felt more like when I was in college selling Fuller Brushes. The product was great, but I was never sure whether the person wanted what I had to offer or just wanted me to leave them alone.

—Richard

I knew Lisa was trying to tell me something important, but I was about ready to move out of town. Finally, I realized what it was. She was pregnant and wanted help. Well, I hooked her up with a few other Christians. But they lived across town, too far away for a teenager to reach easily. And their twice-a-week phone calls just didn't make it.

Three weeks later I heard that Lisa had had an abortion. If only I'd had a solid church close by to plug her into, one that could have cared for her and supported her.

—Julie

My sister and I were raised in a church that didn't preach the gospel. So one day after my conversion—while I was still living at home—I tried to witness to her. I explained why her church activity was inadequate for salvation. She was so offended that she threw my Bible across the hall into my room.

All she experienced was my put-down of something she valued. I had failed to start from a point of her felt need. Nor had I introduced her to something she might want—life in Christ as demonstrated by fellow believers.

—*Mary*

Once on a flight with some clients, I got to talking with one of them about his background, and so forth. He mentioned several things that would have been ideal opportunities for me to share my experience and faith, but I didn't speak up because of the other people there. The opening has never presented itself again, and I don't know quite how to create it.

—*James*

Alice had come over just to chat. I felt kind of pressed with all the things I had to do that day. But I took some time out to go sit in the backyard. The conversation had not turned to spiritual things, but we were getting to know each other pretty well. She seemed eager.

Then the phone rang, and I went in. Gail was asking about the Sunday school committee meeting. I set lunch out for the kids as I cradled the receiver and listened to her "one quick question." The kids arrived home squabbling, so I promised to call Gail back. As I got the kids settled, I realized that I had not yet finished my shopping list for the Friday night church supper. I needed to get the stuff that afternoon because all the next day I was to substitute at the church day care center.

I finished the list about 20 minutes later just as Alice walked in and said, "Guess I'll be going now."

I couldn't believe it; I had totally forgotten her!

—*Jean*

If you are like the average Christian, you've had an experience like one of these. You may truly want to share Jesus with others, but when you hear a glowing report of how someone else did it, you feel a little guilty and wish you could do the same.

Something Missing

Lots of Christian books and workshops are aimed at *personal evangelism.* The equation seems to be: you have a relationship with Jesus Christ + you share Christ with another person = you win a soul for Christ.

There is nothing wrong with this equation per se. At some point in the process of a person coming to the Lord that dynamic often takes place. But it is an incomplete description of what usually happens. It focuses on individuals without understanding that the whole body of Christ in worship, community, and mission *is* a witness to those in need of a Savior. And it is the life together in the body of Christ which has an empowering function, making witnesses of the individual members and creating a light that attracts and informs others.

This book is about that larger picture, the role of the whole church in introducing other people to Christ.

What We Have to Offer

As we face the next century, Carl F. George suggests that the increase in technology and secularism will result in a corresponding longing for greater relationship.[1]

While hospitals are inundated with high-tech hardware, patients are demanding "birthing rooms" and hospice care away from all the tubes and contraptions.

While our society is becoming increasingly secular, New Agers are "thinking peace" on hilltops and aligning themselves with the cosmos.

To these and other trends, the church can respond with more than programs and precepts, more than TV and politics. Christ has entrusted his church with the gospel, and that gospel is the good news that God desires to receive all people into his family—into a relationship with him and a relationship with one another. He desires it so much that he has sacrificed his Son as a substitutionary payment for our sin.

But how is this good news shared? Many of us have become too complacent in our comfortable churches. They may remain stable, a good place to mingle with our friends, but we've gotten the message loud and clear that speaking of religion is not welcome in public. And so we keep Christ to ourselves.

But Are We Even Holding Our Own?

The fact that 40 million Americans claim to be born again means very little except to politicians and the religio-business. Even when a specific church is growing in numbers, we need to ask *how* it is growing. There are three basic ways a church can grow, and not everyone makes the same progress in fulfilling Christ's commission to "make disciples of all nations, baptizing them in the name of the Father and of the Son and of the Holy Spirit, and teaching them to obey everything I have commanded you" (Matt. 28: 19-20).

1. *Biological growth* refers to the new members coming into the church who are the children of existing members.

Actually, our first responsibility is to evangelize our own children. It may be tempting to think that families aren't nearly as important as the adventurous work of spreading the gospel. And yet, Dr. Dennis Guernsey of Fuller Theological Seminary reminds us that many non-Christian Americans came from once Christian families.[2]

Think about that. The church in the Western world is now having to spend the majority of its time and energy *re*-evangelizing people who should have received the faith in their homes. The front line for Christian training is the family. Moses told us, "These commandments that I give you today are to be upon your hearts. Impress them on your children. Talk about them when you sit at home and when you walk along the road, when you lie down and when you get up" (Deut. 6:6-7).

2. *Transfer growth* is the second means of church growth. Many people are pleased as they see the numbers in their congregation increase, but before we get too excited by this kind of increase, we should look a little more closely. It is true that there are too many believers floating around unattached to any congregation. So it is an important work of the kingdom to bring them back into association with a church congregation.

For those people who are direct transfers from other congregations because they have moved, we do an important service. But we are only rearranging the players on the field. We are not even holding our own in terms of keeping pace with the world's mushrooming population.

3. *Conversion growth* is the only form of growth which represents a direct advance for Christ's kingdom. These are men and women whose lives are turned around by Jesus Christ, who acknowledge him as Lord for the first time and desire to become one of his people. How many of the people who have joined your church this past year represent this area? Take a few moments and review all those you can think of. Into which category do they fit? We should plan for and pray for new ways to witness to the people in this third category.

A Willingness to Change

Those who have studied how churches grow—how people are actually and permanently brought into the kingdom—have identified the *desire* to bring new people to Christ and into the church community as one of the most important qualities in effective evangelism.

If people don't really want their church to grow, it won't grow. Actually, few people would ever put it in such crass terms. But there is a price that must be paid in order to bring more people to the Lord. And that price is the willingness to change. Consider the following report from one church:

> Several years ago our church became deeply burdened for evangelism. We read books about evangelism, saw films suggesting new techniques, and sent some of our leaders to take seminars on more effective witnessing.
>
> Our burden was legitimate, our enthusiasm genuine. We found ways to follow up on new people in our neighborhood and others who had expressed some hint of interest in Christian matters. An evangelism committee was formed, and some folks were led to the Lord.
>
> But something far more significant began happening. In genuinely refocusing our vision outward, the Holy Spirit had the opportunity to begin changing us internally—both personally and corporately in some of these areas:
>
> 1. *Busyness.* Our church meetings kept us so busy that we had no time to reach out to nonchurched people.
>
> 2. *Self-sufficiency.* It is usually a virtue for a church body to care for its own so well that no one is in need. But for us, we had no real need for our non-Christian neighbors, and that created an unhealthy barrier.
>
> 3. *Superiority.* It is appropriate to be confident in one's beliefs and practices, but it can be an expression of insecurity to declare that God cannot work in other ways. The Spirit needed to open our eyes to more of God's greatness.
>
> This internal work by the Holy Spirit ultimately produced more church growth than any of the evangelistic programs. It seems rather reminiscent of the experience of the early church. Those believers were to wait for the Holy Spirit to empower them to be witnesses. And it was an outward, miracle-producing power that they received. But think of the internal, corporate revival that became the real hallmark of that community of believers.
>
> The power they received transformed them so that "Everyone was filled with awe.... And the Lord added to their number daily those who were being saved" (Acts 2:43-47).[3]

Sometimes other forms of change are needed, like giving up the ideal of remaining a small, intimate church with one friendly pastor who does all the work.

Four Characteristics of Growing Churches

For many years there was a mystery about what really worked in the area of effective witnessing. Many people offered their pet theories, usually based on how *they* came to know the Lord or what was popular in *their* church tradition. Some of those theories cast the net broadly and drew many in, but they did not stay. Other methods claimed to be focusing on integrity but reached almost no new people.

However, in the last 25 years a great deal of scholarly research has been done on exactly how people come to the Lord and are successfully grafted into the body of Christ. Kevin Springer, the editor of *Commonlife* magazine, identified the following four basic characteristics of growing churches from the wide range of research he reviewed.

> 1. *Growing congregations have strong leaders* who know how to motivate, set a course, analyze and teach, inspire confidence, and build a team.
>
> 2. *Growing churches make evangelism a priority.* While social action and political action are not excluded from the list of important Christian concerns, making the message of salvation known is viewed as central to the Christian life, and other concerns are subordinate to it.
>
> 3. *Growing churches practice discipleship* by incorporating new members through bringing them to a commitment to Christ, baptizing them, and teaching them to live godly lives.
>
> 4. *Growing churches have an understanding of their purpose*—setting concrete, practical goals that help people gauge their success or failure in meeting God's purpose for their body.[4]

The objectives in this fourth characteristic are not primarily in terms of numbers (though if the church is not growing numerically it is dying). But it should be in terms of three primary categories: worship, community, and mission. Without worship there is no relationship to God; without community there is no congregation. Each of these areas builds up the believer *and* provides the foundation for reaching out in mission. And it is these areas that we want to explore further in this book.

The Potential of the Corporate Witness

Consider the following true example of effective witness. Notice the roles played by the corporate ministry of the whole church in terms of worship, community, and mission.

* * *

The harsh grip of the Midwest winter would not let go and the Harpers were having financial problems. Ted and Ann's wallpapering business had been slowly slipping for a long time, eating up their reserves and running them into debt. Surely it would soon pick up . . . but then the bottom dropped out completely.

Their electricity was cut off, they were facing eviction, and they had just had a new baby when Peggy Bradshaw, a member of the church in their neighborhood, discovered there was no food in their house, and the baby was diapered only in a dishtowel.

Some church funds and personal contributions paid the back rent and arranged to have the electricity turned on. Other church people organized to deliver hot meals—a tradition the church members regularly practiced among themselves when a baby was born. They also provided groceries for the Harpers' shelves. And Peggy and Phil Bradshaw's small group began praying regularly for the Harpers.

It took time, but Ted found another job, and the family slowly got back on its feet financially.

To the Harpers, it was a miracle. But how were they to understand it? To many people failure can be a great humiliation, almost the worst thing that can happen. "But," assured Peggy, "failure is no disgrace to the Christian. We don't need to strive for an image of success. Look at the rest of us in this church. Even those who appear quite successful are not afraid to tell you of their weak areas." Then she gave Ann a Bible.

Over the next few weeks the two women met together regularly and discussed the things Ann was reading. Slowly she became convinced that what had happened was not just a generic miracle, but a direct gift from God to their family. Ted was concluding the same thing, and together the Harpers agreed to visit worship services with Peggy and Phil Bradshaw.

At worship that first morning, the Harpers discovered that the people in this church were not mere philanthropists. These Christians really believed the things they had been reading in the Bible during the week.

That afternoon, after a meal together, Ted told Phil Bradshaw he wanted to become a Christian. Together the two men went outside. In one of the first warm days of spring they sat in the yard as Phil led Ted to the Lord.

With joy, Ann reported that she had also become a Christian as she had read the Bible and prayed on her own, but she had not wanted to put undue pressure on Ted.

Soon the Harpers were baptized and included in one of the small groups in the church and are now giving to others.

For Group Discussion

1. Recall a time when you tried to witness, but it didn't work out. Share the experience with others in your group and invite insights on whether and how a stronger church base might have made it more effective.

2. With others in your group, list the people who have joined your church over this past year. How many were the result of biological growth, transfer growth, and conversion growth? What does this say about your church's emphasis?

3. The Mennonite Church has pledged to double its 100,000 membership by 1995. Whether you are a Mennonite or a member of another denomination, what would it cost you personally for your church to accommodate 100 percent growth over the next five years? How would your whole church have to change? Discuss these changes with your group.

4. What would you identify as your church's current objectives in terms of worship, community, and mission? Discuss this with your group to discover your degree of unity.

CHAPTER TWO

Barriers
or Bridges

One day in the midst of his busy Galilean ministry Jesus entered Capernaum. His return to the town where he had already healed and taught made headline news. Pharisees and doctors of the law gathered from every town of Galilee. Some had come even from distant Jerusalem. A crowd formed quickly about the house where Jesus began to teach. Closer and closer to him pressed the people, filling the room and blocking doorways.

Four men carrying a paralytic on a stretcher approached the edge of the crowd. They could get no closer. In vain they tried to elbow a way through the throng. The multitudes, concerned with their own needs or lost in the excitement of the occasion, did not notice the helpless man. Perhaps a few glanced over their shoulders, saw the sick person, but cared too little to help. Jammed together, shoulder to shoulder, in a tight circle around Christ, they formed an unbreakable human palisade, and kept a needy man from the touch of the Healer.

But the four men were determined. Finding their way to the outdoor stairway, they climbed to the flat roof, pried up some tiles, and lowered the stretcher right into the presence of Jesus.

Who Are We?

Usually, in telling the story, we identify ourselves with the four friends whose faith Jesus recognized. But if we could see ourselves truly, we might rather be identified with the thought-less crowd.

It is possible for Christians to press so closely together, preoc-cupied with their own needs and with the joys of togetherness, that they fail to see the needs of their neighbors. Standing shoulder to shoulder, the crowd that clusters around Christ may form a human barrier which keeps others from his healing touch.

What Do Others Think?

To discover how Christians look to others can be a humbling experience. "She doesn't want to have anything to do with me because I don't go to church," one woman commented about her Christian neighbor. "Lots of Christians are like that," she added.

Nor is this an isolated example. Believers often tend to limit the depth of their friendships with non-Christians.

It is surprising to discover how many people have the im-pression that the more committed a Christian becomes, the more withdrawn, unfriendly, and even suspicious of non-Chris-tians they get. Neither is it unusual to overhear Christians, while discussing the sale or rent of a nearby house, express pleasure that their new neighbors will be "church people."

In his excellent book, *Everyday Evangelism*, Tom Eisenman says:

> It is simply not as easy as it once was to relate to others. You don't know what to expect when you knock on someone's door today. Most of the time you can't be positive that the couple living there are mar-ried.... More than any other time in our history, neighborhoods have become a mix of different nationalities, cultures, and unusual modern lifestyles.... Few in our neighborhoods are gutsy enough to stick their necks out.
>
> But Christians have a reason to reach out in love. We have a model in Jesus, who attacked all barriers to relationship.[1]

It's so much easier to jog along in the accustomed ruts if the people next door are people like ourselves. Minding our own religious business, we count ourselves a city set on a hill, without considering that our light may be hidden under a bushel. Would others know how to enter our close circles even if they desired? To break into such tight groups may demand as much boldness as it took the four friends to climb the roof and tear up the tiles. Can outsiders be sure of a welcome when they do enter?

Superior to the Poor?

A young couple, on a short-term mission assignment to take the gospel to migrants, dressed like migrants, worked in the fields with them, and followed the ripening crops. Sharing in the lives of these people, they found friendship and a response to the gospel message. As they moved northward with the harvest they traveled through communities where they weren't known. One Sunday morning they discovered how unready many church members were to receive such persons in Christ.

On that particular Sunday morning they attended services in a pleasant-looking church of their own denomination. But the dubious welcome they received as "migrants" was not convincing evidence that it was a mission-minded congregation, even though its bulletin board proudly displayed pictures of the many foreign missionaries it was supporting.

Scared of the Rich?

Often, though, it's not the poor person who needs the greater boldness. Most of us have taken seriously the warning of James so that we welcome the shabby stranger who ventures into a church building on a Sunday morning. But the well-dressed person may be offered only a cool handshake when he or she visits. If a visitor seems to be rich, highly educated, or of superior social status, it's easy to assume that he or she is a cold observer visiting out of mere curiosity. Yet this person may also be a hungry soul who should be warmly welcomed as a potential member of Christ's body.

More often than we realize, those we regard as casual visitors are seeking for a new reality lacking in their own religious experience. "We're nice to visitors that look like common people," observed a young woman from a congregation in a university town. "But when visitors come from the college, most of us look them over and freeze up. I think we're scared to talk to people who have more education than we have."

In another place, a successful businessman who had just found Christ was looking for a church home. Several Sundays he attended services at a church not too far from where he lived. The members, mostly farmers, gave him a courteous welcome as a visitor, but no one dreamed of inviting him to join their group. Eventually he took the initiative in making an appointment with the pastor to ask, "How can I become a member?"

Why Build Walls?

Sometimes congregations or church leaders deliberately build walls around their fellowship in an effort to protect weaker members. While 99 lost sheep wander in the wilderness, they bottle-feed and blanket the one in the fold. The 99 remain lost, and the pampered one never matures.

Jesus' approach was so different. Consider the company into which he led his disciples—dishonest tax collectors, prostitutes, sinners of every description. This shocked the Pharisees, who believed in erecting high walls of separation.

More often, however, it is our unconscious attitudes that build the high wall that keeps sinners from the Savior. We regard as "good" the Christian who faithfully attends all the church meetings. We commend Christian fellowship as though fellowship were an end in itself. But this is not true. The fellowship to which Christ calls us is purposeful. He prayed that all who believe on him should be one in him, not merely for the joy of togetherness, but so the world might believe in his person and work (Cf. John 17:21).

Bring Them In

The four friends of the paralytic could bypass the crowd by climbing to the roof, but for most people today it is not so simple. The only way modern people can see Christ at work is through his work in the lives of believers. People need to see truth in action before it becomes real to them. Even the chosen twelve needed three years of close association with Jesus in his earthly ministry before they could comprehend the spiritual truths he wanted to teach them.

To understand the love of God for all people, men and women must see love portrayed in Christian relationships—the oneness which recognizes no barriers of wealth, position, education, nation, race, or sex. To be convinced that God was in Christ reconciling the world to himself, they must see Christ in his people, reconciling them to one another as well as to God. Jesus was the brightness of God's glory and the expression of his person. He reflected the nature of God so perfectly that he could declare, "Anyone who has seen me has seen the Father" (Jn. 14:9). In just the same way we are called to reflect Christ's image to the world.

Fellowship Is God's Instrument

As Peter reminded the Christians scattered throughout Asia Minor, we are a people chosen to show forth the praises of God, who has called us from darkness to light (Cf. 1 Pet. 2:9). This is the way God has chosen to reveal himself and to work in the world. His instrument is a fellowship of redeemed people. The isolated witness of many solitary Christians is not enough. It is no accident that in the days following Pentecost, when Christian fellowship was at its warmest, the Lord added to the church daily. Fellowship which truly centers in Christ has drawing power because Christ has power to draw men and women to himself.

A Twofold Purpose

Mark's record of Jesus' choice of the twelve mentions the twofold purpose of that call, "that they might be with him and that he might send them out to preach" (Mark 3:14). The purpose of Christ for all disciples is the same. Together we draw near to him so that from this fellowship we may receive strength to go out to win others.

Telling others about Christ is not an option like dessert after a full meal. It is part of the nature of being Christian. Evangelism must be continuous, not sporadic; not a special emphasis, but the normal pattern of church life. Winning others to Christ is not one of the many duties of the church, nor even its most important task. It is the church's reason for existence.

As Robert Coleman, author of *The Master Plan of Evangelism*, points out: "That some in the fellowship might be excused from service does not even occur as an option in the New Testament. Everyone saw themselves as workers together with Christ in reconciling the world to God."[2]

We Are Responsible

God loved the world enough to sacrifice his Son. His desire is that all might come to a knowledge of that truth. His people are called to share his love and desire. Christ lived, died, and rose again to redeem the world. He has commissioned his disciples to proclaim the truth of his redemption. Those who have accepted Christ as Savior are under His lordship. They have no right to decide whether or not to obey him.

The Holy Spirit's work is to convict the world of its need of Christ. He indwells every believer. As the church submits to the direction of the Holy Spirit, it will labor to bring others to Christ. When we are baptized into the fellowship of the church in the name of the Father, the Son, and the Holy Spirit, we share in the stewardship of the gospel.

We are responsible to God for those who have not heard. Peter felt the compulsion of this responsibility. At the risk of imprisonment, he told the authorities, "We cannot help speaking about what we have seen and heard" (Acts 4:20). Paul, who counted himself debtor to all people, exclaimed, "Woe to me if I do not preach the gospel!" (1 Cor. 9:16). Even in Old Testament times the burden of God's message burned in the bones of Jeremiah so that he could not be silent.

Neither can the church be silent. For the group, as for the individual, to try to save life is to lose it. The congregation which centers its efforts on cherishing its own life, to the neglect of witnessing, will become cold and lifeless. But in contrast, the church that loses sight of itself in love and concern for the lost will experience again, as a group, that abandonment in love brings life. In an article identifying why some churches grow while others stagnate, Stephen Board quoted one prominent pastor as saying: "I believe any church can grow if it is willing to die as a church and be born again as a mission."[3]

The Message to Give

Our message, by its very nature, demands sharing. The bread of life, clutched selfishly, crumbles in the hand and grows stale. Passed freely from hand to hand, it feeds the disciples and the multitudes with whom they share.

What is this message which completely satisfies only as it is shared? Luke recorded these words of Jesus spoken to his disciples after the resurrection, "This is what is written: The Christ will suffer and rise from the dead on the third day, and repentance and forgiveness of sins will be preached in his name to all nations, beginning at Jerusalem. You are witnesses of these things" (Luke 24:46-48).

This was the message that Peter proclaimed to the crowd that wondered or mocked on the day of Pentecost, to the people marveling at the healed beggar near the Beautiful Gate of the temple, to the eager listeners in the household of a Gentile centurion. Paul preached the same message everywhere as he declared before Agrippa and Festus, "I have had God's help to this very day, and so I stand here and testify to small and great alike. I am saying nothing beyond what the prophets and Moses said would happen—that the Christ would suffer and, as the first to rise from the dead, would proclaim light to his own people and to the Gentiles" (Acts 26:22-23).

It's Possible to Get Sidetracked

The message is the same today: that God sent his Son into the world; that Christ died and rose again; that all who repent of their sins and believe in Christ receive forgiveness of sins and power to live a new life. Whatever the circumstances, whatever the approach, this is the central message. If we fail to convey this, we have not fulfilled our mission.

It is easy to get sidetracked on lesser issues. Others may question us about externals. "How does your church differ from other churches?" they want to know. "What are your views on the arms race? What's your stand on abortion? What form of baptism do you use? What kind of music does your church use? What do you think about TV evangelists? Do I have to dress up if I come to your church?" Only rarely does somebody ask, "What, really, do you believe?" or "How can I find God?"

The fault is not with the questioners. The fault is ours if we answer only the questions about externals and do not lead the inquirers on to the heart of the gospel message—redemption provided by God through Christ.

Sometimes *we* are the ones who are too much concerned with externals, to the neglect of our real task. In 1917, during the Russian Revolution, while the communist leaders were meeting in a house in Moscow, the church officials were meeting in another house on the same street. As the leaders of the revolution consolidated their plans for seizing the country, the leaders of the church were discussing vestments.[4]

Today's World Needs the Gospel

Might ours be a parallel situation? Our world seems to be at the brink of a great catastrophe. Levelheaded leaders—not fearmongers—talk realistically about the destruction of civilization and almost total annihilation. In our fear-torn era, we possess the message of eternal hope—promise of a security which does not depend upon the circumstances of physical life. This is not a time to offer stones when someone asks for bread. A testimony to belief in our church's distinctives is not sufficient. Nor is it enough to be known merely as people who live a wholesome life.

Sometimes we need to explain how the new life in Christ should express itself in conduct and attitudes. But comment on our doctrines becomes meaningless babble if divorced from the reality of redemption to which our doctrines give witness. God's grace motivates us. Always, the truth of the gospel centers, not in what people should or should not do, but in what God has done. Otherwise, our witness will degenerate into a pharisaical quibbling about the details of life and practice; and our prayers will slide into self-righteous thanksgiving to God that we are not like other people.

Can We Improve Our Record?

As our frightened world nears a new century, we feel a need for the spontaneous boldness of first-century Christians to proclaim the gospel, our only salvation from sin and fear. Our assignment is in the great commission. We remember the eternal plan of God to unite everything in heaven and on earth in Christ. Looking at our efforts, we feel guilty because of our clouded witness, our lack of real concern, our failure to speak God's message clearly to our neighbors and acquaintances.

We wallow in self-reproach, or assume that the great commission is spoken to persons more talented or better trained than we. Little is accomplished. Is this too pessimistic? Isn't it true that most of us, when we stop to take stock of ourselves, are dissatisfied with the record of our witness for Christ? This we must face honestly before we can remedy the situation.

Often our failure to evangelize is not sheer neglect. We'd like to witness for Christ more consistently, but we don't quite know how. This book is an effort to help ordinary persons, not fluent speakers or persuasive personalities, to see how they can participate in the unending task of the church.

The Task Is God's

To suggest any practical course of action always involves some risk, for we are not building up an institution by clever human devices. In suggesting methods for personal or congregational evangelism we cannot find a complete answer. Constantly we must keep in mind the supernatural nature of our task—the miracle that God uses earthen vessels to contain and to pour out the treasures of eternity.

But He Wants Our Help

We can take steps to allow God to use us more fully. We can begin to break down the walls we have erected, consciously or unconsciously, against outsiders.

"Just a moment!" someone interrupts. "That's not biblical. We're commanded to be a separated people."

Indeed we are. However, it is from the evils of the world, not from its people, that we shall separate ourselves (Cf., 1 Cor. 5:10).

Actually, our separation has more often become withdrawal from people who are not Christians, rather than a purging of our own worldly attitudes. Kenneth Kantzer, the senior editor for *Christianity Today*, has pointed out, "We cannot serve effectively without understanding people—what they think, where they are going, the shape of their dreams, what are their values, what are the structures that channel their living and influence their decisions."[5]

Too few Christians can count among their close friends even one person who does not know Christ. Yet how can we carry God's love to persons for whom we do not care enough to want to be friends? In purely external matters like buying cars or renting apartments all of us prefer the advice of trusted friends to that of casual acquaintances or complete strangers. Can we expect others to take our words on important questions of life and faith if we remain strangers to them? Before they are ready to give us their confidence, haven't they a right to demand that we prove trustworthy as friends?

You Can Begin Now

If you want to be a better witness for Christ, begin immediately by drawing into your circle of close friends one person who is not a Christian. You can form this new relationship on a person-to-person basis, but since your other close friends will soon become involved, perhaps you should tell them your plans. In this first venture it may be wise to seek a friend whose station in life does not differ too greatly from yours. Students can be friends to students, homemakers to homemakers, professional persons to their colleagues. Thus you will avoid the temptation to condescend as though your friendship were a benefit to confer on an inferior, as well as the more subtle temptation to use the new relationship as an outlet for an unconquered desire to climb.

Avoid forcing conversation into spiritual channels. Just be friends. Give invitations to your home; visit, go places, and do things together. Learn the art of small talk. In his book *Everyday Evangelism*, Tom Eisenman says, "We should make small talk our major ministry in our neighborhoods. We need to be willing to give ourselves to people where they are, in the ordinary, everyday task of living. Small talk is the natural language of the reality of everyday lives. We should become proficient in it."[6]

It takes courage to allow your thinking and your way of life to be challenged by a person who is not predisposed to respect your beliefs. Of course, sometimes this will put you on the spot. You won't be able to coast along comfortably with the conscience of the group. It would be far easier to retreat into the favorable cultural climate mistakenly called Christian fellowship and flatter yourself on your separation from the world. Going into the world to witness demands more consecration than going to church or special meetings and listening to sermons even to the point of physical exhaustion.

But going into the world to witness is our task, and for that assignment we have the promise of all power in heaven and earth.

For Group Discussion

1. Think of one situation where you may have caused a non-Christian to think that you didn't want to associate with him or her. Share and discuss it with your group.

2. Discuss with your group whether your church is more likely to welcome the rich, poor, educated, or uneducated. How about combinations: the poor-educated or the rich-uneducated, for example? What are the prejudices that underlie these attitudes?

3. What physical or program barriers might keep certain people from feeling at home in your church? Access and facilities for the handicapped? Dress expectations? An inadequate sound system? Most music too difficult for the uninitiated to sing? Inadequate parking or seating?

4. What would be the specific challenges to your congregation if next Sunday there was a ten percent increase in attendance—all non-Christians? What would you have to do to welcome, teach, involve them?

5. What *issues*—not at the very core of the Gospel—does your church hold that might sidetrack new people? How can you continue to value these convictions as matters of advanced discipleship without putting them out front as the first thing a seeker must trip over?

CHAPTER THREE

Witnessing That Wins

We are people who demand a quick fix for every need. If you're hungry, whether you are in Cleveland or Sacramento, you can get a Big Mac in a minute. Political one-liners are supposed to answer all the tough questions. There are books on one-minute management, one-minute dinners, one-minute parenting—instant answers and solutions to every problem.

It's tempting to approach sharing the gospel in the same way. You are in earnest about your task of witnessing and you turn to the New Testament for guidance. You'd like to find from the lips of Jesus an exact statement of what you are to say about the gospel. To your surprise, it's not there!

Shortly after Jesus called the twelve disciples, He sent them out with these instructions: "As you go, preach this message: 'The kingdom of heaven is near'" (Matt. 10:7). Jesus' own approach was different with different people. To one he said to sell all he had and give to the poor; to another to be born again; to one to go home and not tell anyone what God had done for him; to another, "Follow me." After his resurrection Jesus told the eleven that repentance and forgiveness of sins should be preached in his name among all nations. The great commission states simply, "Go into all the world and preach the good news to all creation" (Mark 16:15).

Not much help in boiling the gospel down to 25-words-or-less or "Salvation in Three Easy Steps."

Not in Memorized Words

Jesus avoided giving such a summary, not because the message is vague, nor because he wanted to mystify us. The gospel is much more than a set of words to memorize and recite, more than a mere system of thought to transmit. Either of these would soon have degenerated into religious gibberish. Christ did not want his followers to be like the Pharisees, worshipers of words and traditions. His message could be fully revealed only in his person, life, and work. Words alone would not suffice.

For instance, when the disciples of John the Baptist came asking, "Are you the one who was to come, or should we expect someone else?" Jesus did not give them a statement to quote. Instead, he invited them to observe for themselves his ministry of healing and teaching and to take their own report back to John.

The truth is that *you cannot give the gospel to others except in terms of what the gospel means to you personally.* Multitudes of robots could be manufactured to transmit a creed for people to memorize, but the living Christ must be shared in terms of human experience. Jesus' choice of the word "witness" to designate the task of his followers suggests this truth. "You will be my witnesses . . ." (Acts 1:8).

What Is a Witness?

Modern courtroom procedure has made us familiar with the term *witness.* A witness is one who has seen, heard, or done something which is relevant to the case and is under obligation to tell truthfully what one knows. Jesus said to his disciples, "You also must testify, for you have been with me from the beginning." For three years these disciples had lived close to Jesus, and in knowing him they had known God. They could say with conviction, because they spoke from firsthand experience, that Jesus was God's Son sent into the world to save all people and that he suffered, died, and rose again.

What Can You Tell?

You and I, however, did not have this firsthand experience with Jesus in his earthly life. Yet we, too, are called to witness. Paul hadn't known Jesus as the twelve had, but he witnessed clearly to the saving power of Jesus' death and resurrection. Paul's unfailing faith was based upon the fact that the Savior, whom he met on the Damascus road, had become to him a real and living person who turned his life around. Christ had forgiven Paul's sins and had given him new life. Christ dwelt within Paul and empowered him to live and witness for God. With Christ, Paul enjoyed fellowship more satisfying than that of any earthly friend. Because he had experienced this, Paul could witness for Christ as convincingly as any of the original disciples.

A similar witness can be given by all who truly know Christ and are living in him. As Robert Coleman, author of *The Master Plan of Evangelism*, points out, "In basic nature, every true Christian is a continuous walking miracle."[1] The miracle of God in our own lives is the story we have to tell.

A Witness—Not a Salesperson

A witness at a court trial is chosen, not for fluent speech or a persuasive personality, but for his or her knowledge or experience which bears on the case. A witness does not need to be a good salesperson. All that is required is to tell truthfully what he or she knows. That is what God requires of us—simply to tell others what we have found in Christ.

Many of us feel hesitant about salesmanship of any kind. We'd be failures as door-to-door peddlers of brushes, books, or vacuum cleaners. We're even more scared to try to sell to strangers anything so unpopular as religion. "Easy-steps-in-soul-winning" books don't seem to make it any easier. But even among salesmen there's an old maxim: "The best advertisement is a satisfied customer." There's not a person among us too timid to show friends the good points of our new car, nor anyone too shy to tell a neighbor about the wonderful stain-resistant carpeting we found on sale. We aren't afraid we're interfering when we do this. Sharing such news is a favor, not an intrusion.

The Power Is the Spirit's

Just being ready and eager to tell what Christ has done for us is far more convincing than argument, reasoning, or successful sales techniques. As Christians, we should respect the other person's right to make his or her own choice. Even the omnipotent God does not coerce; neither should we.

It is not our responsibility to save the world. In fact, we cannot save even one person, nor can we make an individual feel in need of a Savior. That is the work of the Holy Spirit. Conviction which leads to repentance, faith, and conversion is a miracle of God's Spirit which no human scheme or effort can duplicate or guarantee to make happen. The most skillful contact will accomplish nothing if it is merely a two-way conversation. The invisible third party, the Holy Spirit, does the real work.

We can totally rely upon the Holy Spirit to prepare other persons to receive our witness for Christ. We can trust him to lead us to opportunities to testify, to make us sensitive to these opportunities, and to give us readiness to speak. This means that we need to live in intimate and unbroken fellowship with God so that we are continually alert to his guidance. Awareness of this dependence drives us to prayer for ourselves and for those to whom we feel responsible to witness.

Prayer Precedes Witnessing

Usually failure to witness can be traced to failure to pray. Think about the atheist who works at the machine next to yours in the shop, the self-sufficient professional who gives you orders in the office, or the friendly neighbor who just doesn't take time for church. It isn't likely that the Holy Spirit will direct you to begin a conversation about spiritual things with any of these people if you are not already praying for them earnestly and consistently. In fact, unless you have been prepared by prayer, any such contact is likely to be ineffective, if not actually harmful to the cause of Christ.

Evangelistic concern which is not deep enough to compel us to intercessory prayer is too superficial to result in a powerful witness for Christ. This is true whether witnessing to those we know best or to casual acquaintances and strangers. No cleverly devised method or approach can substitute for the unceasing prayer and unbroken fellowship which enables the Holy Spirit to guide us to speak to those whose heart he has prepared for the truth.

"I find that when I am living in close fellowship with God, I do not need to create witnessing situations," testified an active Christian worker. "People hungry for spiritual help come to me."

A Christian homemaker discovered the same truth: "My neighbor was here today. She has been growing cold and in-different, but this afternoon she really opened her heart. I was glad for an opening to talk with her about Christ. I'm at home all day and see hardly anybody. I had been asking the Lord to give me an opportunity to witness for him. Today he answered my prayer."

A Christian nurse said, "One of my patients was scheduled to have a leg amputation the next day. He had refused to let anyone read from the Bible to him and was listed as having no church affiliation. As I was caring for him that morning, he said to me, 'You're a Christian, aren't you?'

"I replied that I was.

"He was silent for a moment, then said, 'Does God really know about me and love me?'

"Rather astonished, I thought a bit and then said, 'You feel as though a good God couldn't let something like this happen if he loved you, don't you?'

"He admitted that he couldn't see *why* this should happen to him. I tried to help him see that what looks like tragedy to us may in reality not be punishment but God's way to change our lives for his better purpose. I then asked if I could read for him from the Bible. I read Psalm 23 and had prayer with him. He has since become a Christian and a friend of ours."

Witnessing at the direction of the Holy Spirit, we can speak with confidence and power because we know the final responsibility rests with him. We need not scatter seed blindly in the vague hope that some will take root somewhere. We have the assurance that God is already calling those to whom he sends us as witness.

Not Superior to Sinners

An awareness of our dependence upon God will keep us from the holier-than-thou attitude which can mar our witness. Paul identified himself completely with his audiences, counting himself chief of sinners and least of saints. We have no reason to feel superior to sinners, for we are sinners too. The only difference is that we have received forgiveness through faith in Christ.

All of us are like the homeowner in one of the parables Jesus told. When friends come to us in the journey of life to ask us for bread, we have nothing of our own to set before them. The only bread we can give is that which we ourselves receive as a free gift from God. We are not rich people inviting the hungry to come to our table. Rather, we are beggars sharing with fellow beggars the bread of life, God's gift to sinner and saint alike. We are not "good" people telling the world about their sins. We, too, often need to confess our sins and ask God's continuing forgiveness.

Throughout all ages the greatest saints have been most keenly aware of their own sinfulness. We have no righteousness except the righteousness which is given to us by God through faith. For this reason we need not wait until we feel worthy to witness. We can freely admit that we have not outgrown temptation, that we continually need cleansing, that we are dependent day by day upon the righteousness of God. The best witness is the one who, like Paul, appreciates the depth of our own need and the riches of God's grace to meet that need. His "power is made perfect in weakness" (2 Cor. 12:9).

Communication Is Two-Way

Only as we keep in mind our oneness with sinners in constant need of grace can we succeed in communicating with those who do not know Christ. Communication implies equality. It is two neighbors talking across the back fence or two co-workers chatting over coffee—not a millionaire condescending to his chauffeur or a corporate president talking down to the mail room clerk. Because communication is a dialogue rather than a monologue, we must be as ready to listen as to talk.

"Is it possible," asks Kent Stickler, vice-president of Financial Shares Corporation in Chicago, and a communications expert, "that God gave us one mouth and two ears as a clue that we should listen twice as much as we talk?"[2]

Frank Laubach, of world literacy fame, learned this truth early in his missionary career. In Lanao, one of the Philippine

Islands, he found an atmosphere of suspicion and violent hatred. Attempts to make friends, even approaches to do business, were rebuffed by brief replies or silent hostile stares. Discouraged and defeated after weeks of effort, he climbed the hill behind his cottage each evening to pray to know God's will. "Often he prayed aloud," recorded his biographer, "and then listened with all his soul for an answer to the prayer. One evening, when his despair was deepest, his lips began to move, and it seemed to him that God was speaking through his own voice.

" 'My child,' the voice said, 'you have failed because you do not really love these Moros. You feel superior to them because you are white. If you can forget you are an American, and think only how I love them, they will respond.

" 'And Frank Laubach answered, 'It is the truth, God. Drive me out of myself, and come and take possession of me and think thoughts in my mind.

" 'And the voice said again through his own lips, 'If you want the Moros to be fair to your religion, be fair to theirs. Study the Koran with them.' "

Learn to Listen

"The next day, when he told some *panditas* that he wanted to study the Koran, they crowded into his cottage eagerly, ready to make him a good Muslim. The man wearing the brightest-colored *malong*, with buttons of ten-dollar gold pieces, brought under his arm a pamphlet which listed the holy books of Islam. He read the titles impressively: the Torah (the laws of Moses); the Zabur (the psalms of David); the Kitab Injil (the Gospel of Jesus Christ); and the Koran of Muhammad.

"Dr. Laubach said as best he could in their language, 'From childhood I have studied the first three books on your list.'

"At once they found that there was much to discuss in their common knowledge. Partly in English, partly in the Moro tongue, the *panditas* talked of Jesus as the holiest prophet after Muhammad, and told how God had carried him up to heaven when he was praying in Gethsemane. Dr. Laubach bit his tongue and did not try to correct them. Instead, he asked questions and found that several Old Testament patriarchs—Abraham, Noah, Jacob, David—were familiar to them under slightly different names."[3]

Realizing after this discussion that he needed to know their language better, Dr. Laubach asked for a language teacher and began the involved task of getting the spoken speech into writing and preparing a dictionary.

The *panditas* and a group of young Moros followed the work with great interest, and Frank Laubach eagerly accepted the opportunity to learn from them more about Muhammad. All during his period of discouragement he had been seeking to learn more about prayer and its power. When he told the *panditas* that he was trying to do the will of God every moment of the day, they said, "Any man who tries to do the will of God all the time is like Muhammad himself. We love to listen to you because you tell us beautiful things from the Koran."

"And he would answer, 'But I learned these things from Jesus.' "[4]

Now the Moros, who just a short time before had rejected Dr. Laubach's offer to open a school, were begging to learn to read. They came in such great numbers that Dr. Laubach was kept busy preparing papers, booklets, and reading charts.

"In the success of the reading campaign, Frank Laubach had not lost sight of his real purpose in Lanao. Reading was not an end in itself, but a means to an end. . . . He did not urge these Muslims to be baptized or to join his church, but they showed a growing interest in the services. Often the windows of the room that served as a church were crowded with faces of those watching from the outside."[5]

Listen to Learn

Like Laubach, all of us need to learn to listen sympathetically as friends, not with the critical attention of a debater listening for flaws and eager to prove his own point of view. We dare not smugly assume that we have nothing to learn, even from unbelievers. To claim perfect knowledge, to fail to admit that we see through a glass darkly, is to claim equality with God. That is the sin that caused Lucifer to fall from heaven.

John Woolman, an early American Quaker, expressed the humility which should characterize the dialogue of all Christ's followers: "A concern arose to spend some time with the Indians, that I might feel and understand their life, and the spirit they live in; if haply I might receive some instruction from them, or they be in any degree helped forward by my following the leadings of truth amongst them."

Listen to Understand

Often we Christians fail to communicate the message of Christ clearly because we are unwilling to listen intently enough to understand another person. Talking long and loud about what we think he or she ought to know, we fail to discover what this person really needs to know. Many times we do not even understand the vocabulary he or she uses and mistakenly assume that the other person understands ours. We use words like *lost, saved, redemption, conversion,* and *faith* without realizing that we are speaking in a foreign tongue.

Missionaries to other lands face the fact that communication involves more than merely translating words into another language. They learn to listen in order to communicate clearly.

"When we speak to children," wrote a missionary to Somalia, "we naturally adapt our words and way of thinking to their level. When we speak to people of other beliefs, customs, thought patterns, and languages, we must adapt ourselves to their way of thinking and expression. More than that, we must understand them out of love. If we do not to some extent become partakers with the people whom we want to lead, our efforts to lead them in worship will often fail because of misunderstanding. . . .

"Recently in our village the police caught a thief and imprisoned him. It was not difficult for the thief to break through the mud-plastered stick walls and make his escape. When the police noticed the escape, there was a rush to the guns; but since the thief was long out of sight, the guns were fired into the blue sky. As policemen they had been trained to shoot at runaway prisoners; and since their target was not in sight, they may have found emotional satisfaction in hearing the report of their guns. If we lack understanding of the people . . . we may level our spiritual guns at an enemy long since vanished out of sight, getting some self-satisfaction from the fact that we are doing something."[6]

Listen to Win

Listening to another person with respect for his or her point of view prepares that person to be willing to listen to you with respect for your beliefs. If a couple Mormons, or Jehovah's Witnesses knock on your door wanting to tell you about their beliefs, your first reaction may be to say coldly, "I'm really not at all interested in your religion." Wouldn't it be better to be interested, to let the visitors tell you what they believe and what it means to them? Listen so carefully that you are able to say back to them what they have told you. Then ask for equal time to tell them what you believe and what Christ means to you.

To do this, you need not be prepared to refute their teaching, but you will need to be prepared to explain your own faith clearly. Trying to prove they are in the wrong would only make them more determined to demonstrate that they are right.

It is interesting to notice that the book of Jude, which is often quoted to justify heated arguments about Christian doctrine and practice, does not advocate debate. Jude exhorted the saints to contend earnestly for the faith, it is true, but this is followed by not a single word about verbal contention. Rather, he encourages Christians to build themselves up in faith, through prayer, love, and hope, as though the most able defense against heresy is not by word but by the strength of personal faith. If we could really believe this, we would be more ready to pocket our spiritual guns and listen to one another.

The Limits of Speech

Sitting in a Hebrew class in Tel Aviv, Israel, Bertha Swarr sensed the limitations of telling as a means of communicating faith. "In these class sessions one feels the caustic, icy chill of the staunch Jew who has been from childhood taught to let the name of Jesus be accursed; and the indifference of the 'free' souls to whom nothing but today matters. And deeper still, one suffers the agonizing longing to share our message, which cannot be done with words until one has first become accepted, trusted, and loved, as a person."[7]

Being, Doing, and Speaking

In witnessing at home, too, we must recognize the limits of verbal communication. We tell by *being* and *doing* as well as by *speaking*. The most effective witness is a balance of life, service, and speech. Only one or two aspects will be partial communication. If *speaking* without *being* and *doing* is hypocrisy, just as truly *being* and *doing* are incomplete without *speaking*. Like a picture without a caption, they may be admired by those who do not understand what motivates Christian life and service. An aged invalid, watching from his cot outside his barrack home in an Austrian refugee camp, assumed, because no one had taken time to explain, that the voluntary workers helping to build houses for resettlement were part of a forced labor project such as he had known under Nazism.

Likewise, when we condemn *doing* without *speaking* and *being* as empty human effort, we must recognize as well that those who try to *be* and to *speak*, neglecting to *do*, are blind to the nature of the gospel, which is deeply concerned with ministering to all of a person's needs, whether physical or spiritual. James rebuked severely those who piously intoned, "Depart in peace, be warmed and filled," and did not care enough to give food and clothing.

While it is hard to imagine really *being* without *doing* and *speaking*, all of us are familiar with the temptation to *speak* and to *do* so much that we have scarcely time left to *be*. We busy ourselves with excellent service projects—building housing in Appalachia, disaster service, volunteering at nearby missions or camps, delivering food gifts to the elderly. And how we speak—in Sunday school, street meetings, youth fellowships, camps, on programs of all types! Yet in all this whirl of talk and activity, we may neglect the importance of *being* Christian— being alone with Christ, bearing one another's burdens in prayer, being friends to those who do not know Christ.

How Good a Witness Are You?

As you seek to draw unbelievers into your circle of friendship within reach of Christ's healing touch, remember also to look within. Is Christ so real to you that you can talk of him as enthusiastically as you praise your new car or carpet? Are you concerned enough about your unsaved neighbors and friends to pray consistently for their salvation? Are you living in such close fellowship with God that the Holy Spirit can direct you each moment? Can you humbly take your place with other sinners as receivers with them of the grace of God? Are you willing to learn from others? Have you really learned to listen? Do your life and service speak to others the same testimony that your lips give?

To become an effective witness is not as easy as memorizing a set of techniques for soul winning (although these are sometimes useful). It is a costly gift, granted to those who are willing to pay the price for spiritual power.

For Group Discussion

1. Divide into groups of three making sure someone in each group has a watch. Go around the circle and "witness" how you came to faith in Christ. Take only three minutes each. Then go around the circle again taking no more than two minutes each to tell how this has made you different than you were or might have been. Or have persons take a few minutes to write out their testimonies to share with each other.

2. Share one area of temptation that you haven't outgrown which allows you to continue to identify with sinners. Try to avoid superficial or benign admissions such as, "I'm not as considerate as I should be."

3. Share the last time you sought a non-Christian's advice. In what ways can we increase two-way communication with non-Christians?

4. What aspects of your faith and life might you first share with a Mormon, a Jehovah's Witness, or a Moonie that might engender some interest rather than immediately challenge his or her beliefs?

CHAPTER FOUR

Who Are the Witnesses?

James Kauffman feels enthusiastic about his pastor and his congregation. "We really have a dynamic preacher," he'll tell you, "and a church built on the genuine New Testament pattern. I suppose you know Brother Kingsley, our pastor? He's getting to be known pretty widely as an evangelist. Can he ever preach a good evangelistic sermon!

"Besides that, he's active in visitation work. He not only calls on his members faithfully, but somehow finds time to visit and witness to the unsaved in our community. He does personal work, too, as he travels. And we really appreciate the kind of guest evangelists he invites into our church. Our winter revival meetings draw crowds from all the churches in our community and visitors from quite a distance."

James then recites a long list of other people who are on the church staff or work in nearby para-church organizations.

"Of course, I'm just an ordinary member," he smiles apologetically, "but I try to be a faithful one. I teach a Sunday school class, though I'm sure others do a better job. I try to do a good job when I'm put on church committees—and that happens pretty often. I do my best to support all our meetings with my presence. There aren't many times I've had to miss a service."

Good for James. We wouldn't want to dampen his enthusiasm and loyalty, but is the pattern he's described a genuinely New Testament model?

What Is the New Testament Pattern?

Traditionally, we rate as "good" the pastor who is active in evangelism. Likewise, we judge as "faithful" the member who attends all the services and helps out with the "church work."

But in doing this, we reverse the New Testament pattern.

The Bible suggests that the major duty of the pastor is to equip the church *members* to do the work of the church and that that work is most often beyond its walls, out in the world. The real task of the members is not in church activities and organizations, but life, witnessing for Christ to those they contact in the ordinary duties of everyday life.

The pastor's responsibility is to prepare church members for this witness, not to do it for them. Paul outlined the true New Testament model to Timothy: "The things you have heard me say in the presence of many witnesses entrust to reliable men who will also be qualified to teach others" (2 Tim. 2:2).

New Testament Pastors

Ephesians 4:12 says that the gifts of leadership were given "to prepare God's people for works of service, so that the body of Christ may be built up." A study of the duties of a pastor as outlined in the letters to Timothy and Titus shows that the New Testament pastor, while not neglecting evangelism, was expected to be concerned primarily with fitting members of their congregations to live, serve, and witness for Christ.

Ray Stedman, author of *Body Life*, says, "Note that neither the apostles and prophets nor the evangelists and pastors-teachers are expected to do the work of ministry, or even to build up the body of Christ. Those tasks are to be done only by the people, the ordinary, plain vanilla Christians."[1]

Out of a study of Ephesians 4:12, Stedman has produced the diagram on the next page showing the duties of leaders and the responsibilities of members, saints.

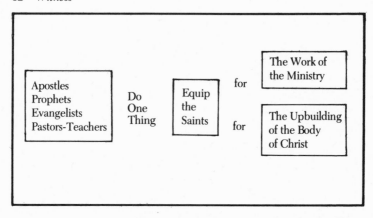

J. Berkley Reynolds, the senior pastor of Good Shepherd Community Church in Scarborough, Ontario, learned this lesson the hard way: "After 13 years, four earned degrees including a doctorate from three different seminaries . . . I was ready to change careers. I was frustrated with programs for evangelism from church headquarters that didn't work."[2] His response? He began meeting with four of his church leaders to begin training them for a ministry of evangelism. Two years later 45 members were hard at work going through the same course—requiring a 16-week commitment. It really is possible to equip the body for ministry.

New Testament Church Members

The picture of activity portrayed in the book of Acts shows that evangelism was certainly not limited to the work of the apostles. Church members must have had a significant part in the spread of the gospel described in Acts, "Now those who had been scattered by the persecution in connection with Stephen traveled as far as Phoenicia, Cyprus and Antioch, telling the message only to Jews. Some of them, however, men from Cyprus and Cyrene, went to Antioch and began to speak to Greeks also, telling them the good news about the Lord Jesus" (Acts 11:19-20). About this spontaneous witness Roland Allen, active in foreign missions early in the twentieth century, wrote:

> I know not how it may appear to others, but to me this unexhorted, unorganized spontaneous expansion has a charm far beyond that of our modern highly organized missions. I delight to think that a Christian traveling in his business, or fleeing from persecution, could preach Christ, and a church spring up as the result of his preaching, without his work being advertised through the streets of Antioch or Alexandria as the heading of an appeal to Christian men to subscribe funds to establish a school, or as the text of an exhortation to the church of his native city to send a mission, without which new converts deprived of guidance must inevitably lapse.[3]

Is Church Work a Superior Calling?

This is not to minimize the need for church organizations and their work. Some Christians are called to preach, teach, exhort, and bear burdens within the church family to prepare and strengthen those who go out to witness. Part of our testimony, too, is the unspoken witness through loving care of the unfortunate—and this service often needs to be done through institutions. It is equally necessary that some take care of the numerous often tedious details involved in sending those who are called far away to witness. All of this is important. An Old Testament story makes it clear that soldiers who look after the baggage are as important as those who fight at the front.

"The share of the man who stayed with the supplies is to be the same as that of him who went down to the battle" (1 Sam. 30:24) said King David. However, in our emphasis on the superior calling of those who serve in church vocations, we tend to exalt the soldiers who "stayed with the supplies" above the ones who "went down to the battle."

Actually, our real battlefront is not in church committees or conferences, but in the secular world where Christian men and women meet daily with those who are not Christian and witness to them. Church vocations and church work are justifiable only as they assist in this witness or enable others to carry it on more effectively. Christians doing a secular job, really living and speaking for Christ there, are fulfilling the great commission. Meanwhile those who are full-time church workers in a church hospital, school, or mission board office or serve as officers or on committees in the local congregation, often find themselves busy with "church work" with little time left for the real work of the church!

Too Busy to Witness

An illustration given by Paul E. Little shows a situation which occurs too frequently among dedicated and sincere church workers:

> A friend recently discussed the whole question of personal witness with me. He has been a Christian for more than twenty years and is a successful businessman with a prominent firm. His work brings him into continual contact with people. He is an earnest Christian, who, in his desire to serve the Lord, felt that he should devote more time to Christian activity, even though he was already very busy. He became an activist, an active one. Night after night he went to rescue missions, children's meetings, and all sorts of other meetings where he spoke or helped in some way. He was so busy in activity that he did not have time for personal fellowship with God. The barrenness of his heart increased with his activity.
>
> When he came to see me, he had begun to think that perhaps instead of going to so many meetings, God wanted him to witness to his next-door neighbors. "But," he said rather desperately, "I don't have any idea of what to say to them. If I invited them into my house, they wouldn't enjoy the things we do; and if I were invited into their home, I wouldn't be able to do some of the things I know they would invite us to do."
>
> Though very successful in his business dealings with people, my friend was at a complete loss when it came to witnessing to his next-door neighbor. And so he took the easy path to isolation, which avoided the problems. It also left his neighbors unevangelized.[4]

Contrast this with the witness given by the church at Rome. "I thank my God through Jesus Christ for all of you, because your faith is being reported all over the world," wrote Paul. To the Thessalonians he said, "The Lord's message rang out from you not only in Macedonia and Achaia—your faith in God has become known everywhere. Therefore we do not need to say anything about it, for they themselves report what kind of reception you gave us. They tell how you turned to God from idols to serve the living and true God." Imagine a modern evangelist coming into a community to preach and finding the audience ready to preach to the evangelist instead because they have been so impressed by the witness of those converted earlier in the evangelist's ministry.

No One Is Called to Observe

Our attitudes too often draw a line between church workers, whether ordained or not, and church members who are assumed to have the right to be passive receivers. This false distinction does violence to the New Testament concept of the entire church as the people of God. The first-century church was not just the business of the apostles, deacons, pastors, and elders. All of the Roman Christians were challenged to present their bodies as a living sacrifice to God.

All members of the church at Corinth were counted members of the body of Christ to do his work. The entire Ephesian congregation was to put on the whole armor of God and take a stand against his enemies. Peter reminded all the Christians scattered throughout Asia Minor that they were chosen to show forth the praises of him who had called them out of darkness into his marvelous light. No member in the church was called to be merely an observer. A congregation was not divided into givers and receivers. Rather, all were to use their special gifts to support and enlarge the witness of the entire group.

The Anabaptist Example

The early Anabaptists, like New Testament believers, recognized the responsibility of every member to join in the witness for Christ. Believing the great commission to be the main task of every baptized believer, they counted all concerns of life—family, work, cultural enjoyments—as secondary to the one great task. They felt that the common person could best witness to common people.

This every-member witness was so effective that enemies of the movement actually feared that the majority of the common people would soon be won by the Anabaptists. In the period from 1551 to 1582, for example, Leonard Bouwens, who had the oversight of congregations in Holland and North Germany, baptized 10,252 persons. "Obviously," commented historian John Horsch, "the greater number of these were not of Mennonite parentage but were won through special effort put forth by local congregations."[5]

How the faith spread through the everyday witness of ordinary people is illustrated by the conversion of Jan Block, as told in *Martyrs Mirror*.

> He associated with a brother named Symon van Maren, a furrier ... with whom he formerly was wont to go to the tavern to tipple, but who, after he was converted, admonished him to read the New Testament, which advice he also followed; and the good Lord so opened his heart, that he understood from it what was right, and joined the church of God. This done, he could not remain hid, since he led a better life than before.[6]

The records show that the Anabaptists did not wait for ordination to preach the Word of God. "Hans Misel, a weaver, who was yet a young man ... was asked by some persons to read and speak from the Word of the Lord; and as he declared to them the way of the truth, he was betrayed and reported."[7]

Indeed, the accusation of teaching without authorization was hurled often against those on trial for their faith. "We say that you are a teacher, and that you seduce many," the lords told a woman identified only as Elizabeth.[8] "Who has authorized you to assemble the people, to teach them?" they demanded of two men arrested in West Friesland.[9]

"Why do you trouble yourself with the Scriptures; attend to your sewing. It seems that you would follow the apostles; where are the signs which you do?" they asked Lijsken in the prison at Antwerp.[10]

Thus, men and women, of all occupations and social classes, continued to teach and testify wherever they went, even though that witness almost certainly meant torture and death.

"Dear mother, can you not think what you please, and keep it to yourself?" asked a sympathetic visitor of the imprisoned widow Weynken. "Then you will not die."

But Weynken replied simply, "Dear sister, I am commanded to speak, and am constrained to do so; hence I cannot remain silent about it."[11]

Advantages of Every Member's Witness

Actually, church members, now as then, are in a unique position for witnessing. The ordinary business of living brings them into contact with all kinds of people—people whom preachers and full-time church workers do not often meet except through forced contacts. Besides this, most unchurched people pay more attention to what a church member has to say. When a preacher comes to call, the non-Christian assumes the talk will be about religion just because that's the preacher's job. When a friend, a neighbor, or a fellow worker talks about Christ, that's something different.

Eleanor quit coming to church after she married Glenn, an unbeliever. When the pastor called on the young couple, the pastor was put off by the cool reception. But some of Eleanor's young Christian friends weren't so ready to give up. They decided to visit as a group. But would Glenn be offended? In the past he had said some harsh things about the church. Ronald who worked with him decided to test him out: "Say, Glenn, my sister and some of the other women would like to visit Eleanor some time next week. Will she be at home Thursday evening?"

"Sure!" was Glenn's quick reply. "We'll stay home if we're going to have visitors. Say, Ronald, why don't you come along so I'll have some company, too?"

To everyone's surprise, the door that was closed to the pastor was still open to the youthful church members who began their witness with nothing more than an offer of renewed friendship.

The Secular Is Sacred

When church members fully understand that their daily contacts give them unique opportunities for witness, they will begin to see that their secular occupations are not secular at all. They will recognize that service to God is not only what they do when they go to church, but also what happens when they meet non-Christians on the job or in neighborhood contacts. Christianity will no longer be just pious faces worn on Sunday, but an everyday thing.

Those who understand this truth cannot have two sets of values—one to talk about soberly in Sunday school and one to live by on the job. Nor will those who recognize the challenge of every day's contacts ever feel that they are doing their whole duty to God when they take time out from "secular" occupations and withdraw from the world to go to church.

Perhaps the most glaring example of assuming that our primary duty to God is to keep busy going to church can be seen in the way we flock to meetings. We confuse doing the work of evangelism with being spectators at meetings.

It is true that Christians are needed to assist in prayer, counseling, or bringing to the meetings those who need to hear the gospel. Usually, however, the person who really needs the message is the last one we think of taking with us.

Too often we unconsciously act like Elaine, a Sunday school teacher who invited a friend to go with her to hear a popular evangelist. Her friend was busy with other church activities and couldn't go, but she suggested, "Why don't you ask Ruth?"

Ruth was a "fringe" church member. And Elaine hesitated. "I'm not sure I want to. Some of the things I've heard about Ruth don't sound too good. If she wants to live that kind of life, I'd rather not have too much to do with her."

Apparently Elaine did not understand that by friendliness with one person who needed help, she would have been assisting in the work of evangelism far more than by taking another Sunday school teacher to hear an evangelistic sermon she didn't need.

No Levels of Discipleship

As we realize that the most effective challenge of the church to the world occurs in everyday life when church members witness faithfully, we will not think of the members as living on a lower level of discipleship than full-time church workers. No longer will we blame second-class citizenship for our passivity, waiting for the pastor to coax, warn, and pamper us.

Together, as we understand the true nature of the church, the pastor and the members will labor to find ways by which we all can give a maximum witness to the world.

Working Together for God

This may, in many congregations, mean organizing evangelistic activities in which members can participate. Whether or not an organized plan for evangelism is introduced, ministers and church workers must, above all, help the members think through ways of making their everyday contacts count for Christ. This involves, in addition to teaching sound Christian principles, helping people to see how these principles apply in daily relationships.

If such suggestions are to be really relevant, church leaders must be ready to listen, to let the members talk freely about the problems and opportunities they meet as they live, serve, and speak for Christ. For instance, what are the problems faced by Christian students in public high school or in college? What opportunities for witness by life, service, and speech present themselves? How can the church best prepare a young Christian to make the most of these opportunities? How can a church member be salt, light, and leaven in factory, office, store, or hospital?

An industrial psychologist whose work is counseling with other workers about their problems on the job, feels that most people check their religion at the door when they come to their daily work.[12] How can a Christian take Christ along to the job? What are ways in which a farmer, a homemaker, or any person who often works alone, can give a witness for Christ?

Thinking through these questions, the pastor and the members will see the gap between their ranks closing. They will find themselves working together as coach and team—one suggesting, encouraging, criticizing, and inspiring; the others doing their best—on the field.

Help in Preparing for Witness

Giving people a sense of confidence that they can competently reach out to their non-Christian acquaintances can sometimes be aided by various training programs.

At Tri-Lakes Chapel in Bristol, Indiana, the members come from a wide variety of backgrounds. Dale Stoll, the pastor, feels the only way to knit a hodgepodge group into a body is to give them a solid biblical foundation. The church was strong on nurturing, Dale realized, but there was not much training for ministry.

Tri-Lakes adopted as their motto T.E.A.M.: Training Every Adult for Ministry. And the method of training they chose is to use *The Bethel Series* to provide the biblical foundation.

The Bethel Series is an overview of the Scriptures which is widely used by many different churches and denominations. Dale Stoll is instructing 15 students in the two-year program who will in turn teach others. It gives them a biblical foundation, and at the same time is leadership training. Some will turn around and teach *The Bethel Series* to others; some will lead small groups.

Dale is excited about *The Bethel Series* and the solid biblical foundation it provides. "I feel like I'm doing what a pastor should do: equip the saints who will in turn go out to minister."

Must I Have the "Gift" of Evangelism?

Many people claim that they do not have the gift of evangelism, implying that they are not equipped to share their faith with non-Christians. Actually, there may be many people with the gift of evangelism who just haven't discovered or developed it yet.

But Peter Wagner, professor of church growth at Fuller Seminary School of World Mission, has defined a spiritual gift as "a special attribute given by the Holy Spirit to every member of the body of Christ according to God's grace for use within the context of the body."[13] And he claims that every believer has one or more spiritual gifts, but no one has all the gifts. Some Christians, it is true, do not have the gift of evangelism.

However, he points out that spiritual *gifts* are distinct from the several Christian *roles*. A Christian role is something we are all to fulfill. We all must exercise the role of faith in order to live the Christian life. But some people have an extraordinary gift of faith. We are all to be hospitable, but some have a special gift of hospitality that is exercised more easily. We all are to pray; some have a special gift of intercession. "A few," says Wagner, "have the gift of evangelist, but all Christians are expected to exercise their role of witness."[14]

Before Jesus returned to heaven, he assured his followers, without exception, that "you will receive power when the Holy Spirit comes on you; and you will be my witnesses" (Acts 1:8). Peter advises us: "Always be prepared to give an answer to everyone who asks you to give the reason for the hope that you have. But do this with gentleness and respect" (1 Pet. 3:15).

Are you willing to pray earnestly that such a readiness and sense of personal responsibility will emerge among the members of your congregation? Are you willing to let it begin in you?

For Group Discussion

1. List the major responsibilities of your pastor (or senior pastor). Place an "e" by each that represents the pastor's role as an *equipper*. Place a "w" by each one where the pastor is expected to be the *doer* or witness on behalf of your church. Discuss whether your church could benefit from some responsibility adjustments.

2. Is there a distinction between clergy and laity in your congregation? Discuss the pros and cons of those distinctions and what would be required for effective change.

3. What advantage do you see in the concept: "Every-member witness?"

4. Discuss the last time your church had an evangelistic service. How much effort was put into getting Christians to attend versus non-Christians.

5. What are some ways that a person who works alone most of the time (like a homemaker, or a farmer) can be an effective witness.

6. This chapter makes a strong case for pastors to equip members for evangelism. To what extent do you think pastors themselves should be involved in direct witness activities?

Witness: Worship

In worship the church enters into God's presence and opens itself to the source of its being. Through Scripture, prayer, proclamation, music, silence, and other spiritual disciplines persons are shaped and formed into a faithful covenant community by the story of God's acts in human history, their experience of God's love and power, and their hope in the coming reign of God.

CHAPTER FIVE

A Foundation for Witness

"The thing I like to do most is to worship God with other believers. To me, it's like going home. It builds me back up after I've been beaten down. There's spiritual reinforcement in praising God with others who also derive their strength from God. It puts life in a new perspective. Even life's hard times are transformed into sources of strength and refreshment.

"To tell the truth, I would rather spend one day in church than live the rest of my life in some fancy resort."

Sound a little fanatical?

Some might think so if they haven't experienced the kind of a worship service that truly gives life. But these thoughts were the opinions of the writer of the eighty-fourth Psalm. It's a common theme in the Psalms. David said,

> One thing I ask of the Lord, this is what I seek: that I may dwell in the house of the Lord all the days of my life, to gaze upon the beauty of the Lord and to seek him in his temple (Ps. 27:4).
> I rejoiced with those who said to me, "Let us go to the house of the Lord" (Ps. 122:1).
> From you comes the theme of my praise in the great assembly; before those who fear you will I fulfill my vows (Ps. 22:25).
> I will give you thanks in the great assembly; among throngs of people I will praise you (Ps. 35:18).

You would think he had found some rare elixir, some transforming fountain of strength and wholeness. And, as a matter of fact, he had. Richard Foster, the author of *Celebration of Discipline* says, "To worship is to experience reality, to touch Life. It is to know, to feel, to experience the resurrected Christ in the midst of the gathered community. . . . If worship does not change us, it has not been worship. To stand before the Holy One of eternity is to change."[1]

If our witness to the world is to have any power and integrity, we need the renewal that can only come through worshiping God together.

Witnesses Need Worship

The original twelve disciples, you will recall, were gathered together in the presence of Christ, learning who he was, being refined in the fire of his example and his teachings, that he might send them out among the people to preach. Any effort to witness to the world must be deeply rooted in a close worshiping fellowship with Christ and with other believers.

This is true because witnessing takes a Christian into the heat of the conflict with the powers of darkness. Being in the world but not of the world makes the church the target of forces opposed to God.

While it is important that Christians maintain friendly communication with those who do not know Christ, it is equally essential to remember that the world is a dangerous place for Christ's followers. Jesus made this clear in his last days with his disciples: "If the world hates you, keep in mind that it hated me first. If you belonged to the world, it would love you as its own. As it is, you do not belong to the world, but I have chosen you out of the world. That is why the world hates you. Remember the words I spoke to you: 'No servant is greater than his master.' If they persecuted me, they will persecute you also. If they obeyed my teaching, they will obey yours also" (John 15:18-20).

The Continuing Conflict

Periods of persecution dramatize the conflict between the forces of evil and the followers of Christ. In such times no Christian is allowed to forget that Satan is trying to overthrow the work of God. Before their deaths two sixteenth-century martyrs expressed in prayer the reality of their struggle:

> We might well have peace with them, if we would not confess thy holy name, and not believe on thy Son, that he atoned for us on the cross, bore our sins, and paid our debt. The enemy has no other reason for his daily raging against us, than because we do not fulfill his will, but love thee, O God, in our hearts, which neither Satan nor his adherents can endure. Therefore they compel us with great distress, and afflict us with much tribulation. Thus, our misdeed, on account of which the enemy fights so hard against us, is that we place our hope in thee alone, and in thy dear Son Christ Jesus, and in the Holy Ghost; therefore we must suffer reproach, because we do not set ourselves against thee; if we would give ourselves up to idolatry, and practice all manner of wickedness, they would let us live unharmed, in peace and tranquillity.[2]

In many places around the world today, Christians are not permitted to forget that Satan's forces are still at war with the children of God. In some places, the very fact of being Christian invites the anger of a God-rejecting society. In some of our own cities and neighborhoods, witnessing Christians encounter antagonism expressed in hostility, disdain, or indifference.

More Subtle Warfare

The conflict most of us face, however, is far more dangerous than open hostility. When society shows a friendly face to the church, Christians may gradually, almost imperceptibly, slip into the world's pattern of life. The salt loses its savor and the light is dimmed as Christians, called to tell the world about Christ's power to save, discover that we have nothing to say. Except for little pockets of time reserved for churchgoing, we spend our days as unbelievers do—climbing the ladder of success, complaining about politics or co-workers, living for weekends and summer vacations, buying the latest in home entertainment, or attending the latest workshop in money-management, assertiveness, or body-building.

How can we proclaim Christ's power to save when we are as worried, prejudiced, frightened, or bored as our unsaved neighbors? How can we testify that Christ is Lord of all when, like those who do not call themselves by his name, we idolize wealth, convenience, comfort, or social status? Words about abundant living in Christ are meaningless on the lips of those whose lives do not differ in quality from the lives of unbelievers (apart from a few things we "don't do because we are Christians"). Phillips' translation of Romans 12:2 points up the subtle danger that threatens Christians in the world: "Don't let the world around you squeeze you into its own mold, but let God remold your minds from within."

Life in Two Spheres

Because of the inescapable danger of life in the world, Christians need to regularly retreat in order that we may return to it with renewed strength, wisdom, and courage to witness for Christ. Worship shared with other Christians, as well as daily personal worship, provides this renewal. As disciples of Christ we live in two spheres—the world's battlefield where we witness for Christ and serve in his name, and the fellowship of the church where we receive the spiritual power which sustains us in our work and witness in the world.

Those who take most seriously their responsibility to witness feel most keenly the need for renewal through worship together. Emptied, weakened, or discouraged by the struggle, they return expectantly to the source of fullness, power, and boldness. Members of a colony of heaven in a hostile country, they are drawn close to one another by awareness of common danger and need for mutual support. A real feeling of need, not merely a sense of duty, makes them regular participants in church worship services.

The Rhythm of Worship and Witness

Our situation today is no more challenging than the one facing the first church. In Acts 3 and 4, we see how those called to witness returned to the fellowship of the church for renewed boldness and power. A lame man had been healed in Christ's name; Peter and John preached Christ to the amazed people who gathered. The crowd at the temple gate attracted the notice of the religious authorities, who had Peter and John imprisoned overnight and brought for trial the next day. The undaunted apostles took their trial as another opportunity to witness for Christ. Boldly they refused to obey the command to stop teaching in the name of Jesus.

When the leaders released Peter and John after a rebuke combined with a threat, the disciples went directly to the gathering of believers. There they told everything that had happened, including the command to be silent and the threat of punishment if they continued to preach Christ. United in prayer, the believers laid the situation before the Lord and asked, not for freedom from persecution, but for greater boldness and power to witness and work for Christ. The result was a new infilling of the Holy Spirit so that they spoke the Word of God with boldness. With the renewed zeal for witness came a deeper sense of unity among the believers.

This rhythm of gathering to receive power, and then scattering to witness, pictures the normal pattern of life for servants of God. The church at worship shares with one another and brings to the Lord the concerns, problems, and triumphs encountered in the work of witness. The church in witness goes forward in the strength gained from worship. Evangelism and worship go hand in hand. One cannot be meaningful without the other.

A Twentieth-Century Example

The rhythm of witness and retreat to fellowship is illustrated by one of the German students who lived in the Christian community of Finkenwalde under the leadership of Dietrich Bonhoeffer. In the hostile atmosphere of Hitler's regime, these future pastors, liable at any time to punishment by the Nazi government for their faith, nevertheless maintained a courageous witness. Recalling those days, Paul Busing wrote:

> Usually we went out in apostolic companies, two by two, staying with folk who were willing to act as hosts. During the morning we went from house to house, visiting people, talking to them, inviting them to an evening meeting in the local church or in a hall. Sometimes afternoon meetings were arranged for women or for children, but the evening gatherings were for all who cared to come. At these meetings we spoke of what was involved in leading a Christian life as a farmer or a teacher, as a merchant or a laborer, as a parent or a child, in Nazi Germany. We tried to help people see that the Christian life means carrying Christ's cross with him and in his discipleship, and that only by following him can we be of his flock.
>
> The brethren who remained at Finkenwalde undergirded us evangelists with their prayers and supplications; when people became aware of this they caught a glimpse of the common life of Christians manifest in a preaching, teaching, and praying church. Nor did we evangelists underrate the importance of a spiritual home to which we could return for new strength and inspiration, for a deeper understanding of God's Word and of the obligations it laid upon us.[3]

Worship That Renews

How can our church worship services provide Christians with the resources we need for successful witness and work in the world? We cannot improve on the fourfold group experience of the first church in Jerusalem, described in Acts 2:42: "They devoted themselves to the apostles' teaching and to the fellowship, to the breaking of bread and to prayer."

1. The Apostles' Teaching. As they gathered for worship, the earliest Christians welcomed every occasion to learn more about the new faith they had received. The apostles, who had first known Christ, were their teachers. What the apostles taught is the message of the New Testament. Their teaching centered on the twofold truth of God's redemption and people's response. They emphasized the fact that God was in Christ reconciling the world to himself. From the Old Testament Scriptures they showed that the death and resurrection of Jesus was according to God's plan for people's redemption. They taught, also, the doctrine of the Holy Spirit's indwelling and empowering all who believe. They explained clearly how a person should respond to God's redeeming love by faith which produces an obedience permeating all of life.

This is the food upon which the flock of God in every period of history and in every place on the globe needs to be fed. The New Testament pastors had only the Old Testament Scriptures on which to build, together with the body of teaching handed down orally by the apostles. Today's pastors and teachers have the apostles' teaching in the written Word of the New Testament. "Preach the Word," is God's command to Christian pastors. To the church he says, "Like newborn babies, crave pure spiritual milk, so that by it you may grow up in your salvation" (1 Pet. 2:2). Preaching the Word includes explaining biblical truth and showing how it expresses itself in life and witness today. Such preaching plays an important part in equipping believers to do God's work in the world.

2. Fellowship. The first church gathered for fellowship as well as to hear the apostles' teaching. Fellowship as practiced in the New Testament seems to have been more than being in the same place and listening together to the Word of God. It meant exercising the privileges and responsibilities of new relationships in the family of those who believed in Christ. Reminders scattered throughout the epistles show that they gathered to contribute as well as to receive.

Advice given to the Hebrews suggests that mutual encouragement was one of the activities of the meeting of Christians: "Let us consider how we may spur one another on toward love and good deeds. Let us not give up meeting together, as some are in the habit of doing, but let us encourage one another" (Heb. 10:24-25). Singing together was an opportunity to testify to one another and to praise God (see Col. 3:16). Fellowship included confession, not only to the Lord, but also to one another (James 5:16). As illustrated in Acts, fellowship meant sharing problems, victories, and experiences in witnessing, which became the subjects of petition or praise in group prayers.

Some churches have "testimony meetings" which usually means getting up and sharing with others how you became a Christian. But at Reba Place Church, in Evanston, Illinois, a "sharing time" is a regular part of each worship service. The emphasis is on sharing how God has worked in one's life *this week*, to give praise or to ask for prayer. In a recent worship service, one man said it was the anniversary of his being released from prison and taken in by this church. An elder shared about the death of his mother, and the witness of her life. A group of giggling junior high girls got up together to thank their youth leaders for all the "neat activities" they'd been having this year. A single woman asked prayer for her brother who was going through a divorce.

These sharings are an opportunity for the entire congregation to participate in the joys or help carry the burdens of a brother or sister. They also are a witness to visitors that God is at work in the lives of his people, gathered or scattered.

3. Breaking of Bread. It seems that the first church broke bread together as part of their regular worship. Evidently they did not fear that too frequent communion services would make the breaking of bread seem commonplace. Did they feel, rather, that they could not be reminded too often of the redeeming love of Christ and of his promised return?

Remembering God's redemptive act stimulated joy and gratitude which found expression in praise, thanksgiving, witness, and service. Anticipating his return kept them from being chained by earthly interests, ambitions, and cares. As they rested their happiness on their hope in Christ, they rejoiced in persecution and the loss of earthly possessions.

As Christ's disciples today, might we be less chained to earth and more ready to respond to every call of God if we more frequently remembered Christ's atoning death and his promise to return?

4. Prayers. Prayer was the fourth exercise of the early church gathered for worship. "Of all the words for prayer [in the original language] the one used here is at once the most exclusive and the most inclusive: the most exclusive in that it represents prayer offered only to God, being a sacred word; and the most inclusive in that it embraces all the exercises of the soul which can be denominated prayer. Adoration, confession, petition, and thanksgiving: all are included in 'the prayers.' "[4]

Like fellowship, the prayers of the first church seem to have been characterized by greater freedom than is common today. Abuse of this privilege of speaking and praying as led by the Spirit caused confusion in the church at Corinth, which Paul rebuked. His correction suggests the type of gathering which was common: "What then shall we say, brothers? When you come together, everyone has a hymn, or a word of instruction, a revelation, a tongue or an interpretation. All of these must be done for the strengthening of the church" (1 Cor. 14:26). He then recommended that any exhortation or prayer in tongues should be interpreted and that members should speak in turn and with respect for one another. But it was definitely participatory, led by the Spirit and not just an "order of worship."

Sunday Morning Worship

As we evaluate our usual worship services, how do we measure up against the fourfold pattern of the New Testament church? Are we emphasizing the "apostles' teaching" to the neglect of fellowship, breaking of bread, and prayers? Often our service centers around a sermon. Rarely is there any spoken exchange among the worshipers; mutual encouragement like that described in the New Testament has little, if any, part. Instead, the speaking is done by one or two persons only, with the assumption that the others are participating by silent inner response.

The breaking of bread or the Lord's Supper is reserved for a special occasion. Prayers, as a rule, are spoken by the pastor or a person selected beforehand, and the congregation is assumed to be praying silently with the leader. By being commonly designated as "opening" or "closing," prayers are relegated to a secondary position.

It is true that smaller groups in the congregation—Sunday school classes or youth groups, women's or men's fellowships, home Bible studies or small "kinship" groups—provide for mutual encouragement and freedom in prayer. Churches are learning how important small groups are—not only for training, building up, and renewing the saints for ministry, but also for drawing in, befriending, and discipling those who are being won to Christ.

Yet shouldn't the congregation as a whole have the privilege of sharing together in all of these four building exercises? This would mean radical changes in the pattern of the Sunday morning meeting in many congregations, since Sunday morning is the only time most congregations gather as a group. But it could be worth it in making worship a balanced experience that brings us into the presence of the Lord in a way that truly renews and refreshes.

For Group Discussion

1. How have you been strengthened in your Christian life and for witness by worship? Share one such experience as specifically as possible.

2. How is the fourfold group experience of the first church as described in Acts 2:42 experienced in your church?

3. What aspects of the fourfold group experience could use enhancement? How? What would have to change to make this possible?

4. Why do you think worship is a renewing experience for the Christian? What takes place that makes any difference?

CHAPTER SIX

The Content of Our Witness

In the same way that worship can be the source of renewal and refreshment for believers, it can also symbolize life and wholeness for the unbeliever. One of the first works of the Holy Spirit in a person's life is conviction of sin. Many times this takes the simple form of opening the person's eyes, removing the delusion that life without God is okay. That's when life with God first begins to have some attraction.

"After a failed marriage, I had two kids and no place to go. But at the first worship service I attended, there was a play based on Leo Tolstoy's story, 'Where Love Is, There Is God Also.' It was about a shoemaker who was looking for Christ and found him in the poor people who came to his door. I was very touched by this and felt a loving welcome.... After about two months I accepted Christ as my Savior and in a few more months was baptized."[1] This is part of the testimony of a single parent who began to catch a vision of the goodness of life with God simply by being in a worship service.

Strengthening its members for personal witness is only a part of the power of Christian worship. The assembly itself, if it is truly under the control of Christ, possesses within its life the power to attract others to Christ. In the drawing power of Christian worship lies one of the greatest resources of the Christian church for evangelism. "When I came into the silent assemblies of God's people," testified seventeenth-century

Quaker Robert Barclay, "I felt a secret power among them which touched my heart; and as I gave way to it, I found the evil weakening in me and the good raised up."

Therefore, in two tangible ways worship and witness are inseparable. On one hand, we have seen in the last chapter that a cup poured out on behalf of others will soon be empty unless it is continuously refilled. For this reason we need to come together in worship with our brothers and sisters in Christ to be renewed for tasks outside the church walls.

On the other hand, the congregation in worship *is* part of our witness. Like Andrew who brought his brother Simon into the presence of Christ, and like the woman at the well who brought her friends and relatives to see a man who knew her better than she knew herself, sometimes the most effective thing we can say is, "Come and see."

What Will People See?

One of the most dramatic worship events ever recorded was the one that the apostle John witnessed and recorded, beginning in chapter 4 of the book of Revelation. Try to imagine what he saw. You may be off in some details, but you can't possibly overdo the magnitude and scope of the scene. So let your mind stretch.

A great throne encircled by a rainbow, and in front of it is what looks like a sea of glass, clear as crystal. Hovering around the throne are strange and wonderful creatures from all over the universe. They are magnificent beings. Are they from other planets, other dimensions? Who knows? They're far beyond Steven Spielberg's wildest dreams. Yet they are part of God's good creation.

Then you notice that seated on 24 smaller thrones, in an arrangement of unusual honor around the central throne, are 24 humans dressed in white with golden crowns on their heads.

You are awed by the strong, loving lines of character that show in their faces. They are the elders.

Somehow you are afraid to look directly at the one on the great throne. It is easier to watch how the others are responding to him.

And their behavior is most revealing. The hovering creatures repeatedly say, "Holy, holy, holy is the Lord God Almighty, who was, and is, and is to come." And every time they do that, the 24 elders fall down before him who sits on the throne and lay their crowns before him in worship.

After a time you become aware of other beings, high and almost out of sight. They are angels, millions of them so that their chorus is almost greater than you can stand.

Across this august stage are marched the kings of the earth, the princes, the generals, the rich, and the mighty. But they are not standing tall and proud in this setting. And soon there appears before you a huge multitude of people wearing white robes and holding palm branches in their hands. There are more people gathered there than you have ever seen at any football game or political rally or on any news report, more than you could ever count.

And that's only the beginning of this great worship service.

Such a worship service would be awesome, and our earthly rehearsals seem feeble in comparison. But in our own churches we can experience the same elements in ways no unbeliever can miss. For instance . . . .

Our God Reigns

It is difficult to actively worship that which we do not truly believe in. People can passively watch or listen to a lot of things, but it is hard to sing your heart out or fall on your face or do other "undignified" things unless you truly believe that you are in the presence of someone so great that the preservation of your own dignity is irrelevant by contrast.

The message here is that God is! He truly exists, and he actively reigns over all creation. That's what the 24 elders were declaring: "You are worthy, our Lord and God, to receive glory and honor and power, for you created all things, and by your will they were created and have their being."

In today's world that declaration is in resounding contrast to modern secularism. "Secularism," says David Wells, "assumes there is no moral or transcendent order related to what we do and before which we are accountable. Secular people are not theoretical atheists, for the overwhelming majority believe in the existence of God. They are, however, practical atheists, for they live as if God did not exist."[2]

Worship declares just the opposite. Not only does God exist, but I am called to deal with him as the God who actively reigns over the universe, the God over me.

There are a variety of legitimate worship styles, but no outsider can experience a genuine worship service where the small and the great, the old and the young, the educated and the ignorant are all worshiping God without getting the shocking message that these people actually believe he is real.

Sin Separates

In John's Revelation the kings of the earth, the princes, the generals, the rich, and the mighty who all marched before the throne had something to say, too. In spite of their exploits on earth, they had come to realize that they were unworthy sinners. They begged the rocks and the mountains, "Fall on us and hide us from the face of him who sits on the throne and from the wrath of the Lamb! For the great day of . . . wrath has come, and who can stand?"

When we are together in worship, this is our message, too. We stand boldly declaring that there is a judge who stands over us and the whole human family.

Today the prevailing point of view is that there is no truth that is true for everyone. "You do your thing, and I'll do mine." This subjective outlook, which denies that there is any real right or wrong, is based on the assumption that there is no judge.

Many Christians who go to church and may *personally* obey most of God's commands have nonetheless lost the courage to call anything sin. It's become bad manners to use the word in polite company. "Don't lay your trip on me, and I won't lay my trip on you," is the public rule.

But vital, corporate worship makes another statement. Together we declare that someone stands above us all whose laws are holy and to whom we *are* accountable. Why else would we pray for forgiveness? Why else would anyone have the courage to make a public confession? Why else would we sometimes weep over sin? It's illogical to behave in those ways if one is only dealing with matters of personal taste, mistakes in practical wisdom, or small indiscretions.

Who should fall on their face for any of that? You just learn what works best—*for you*—and go on. But the Christian worshiper proclaims something more. By their worship they assert that there *is* a heaven to be gained and a hell to be shunned.

Jesus Is the One Who Saves

The great multitude in John's vision that was so impossible to count—the people in white robes and waving palm branches all around—had one resounding theme: "Salvation belongs to our God, who sits on the throne, and to the Lamb." It split the heavens like lightning and caused the earth to quake.

In Revelation 19:6 and 7, John reported the response of all God's servants, both small and great:

> Then I heard what sounded like a great multitude, like the roar of rushing waters and like loud peals of thunder, shouting:
> "Hallelujah! For our Lord God Almighty reigns. Let us rejoice and be glad and give him glory! For the wedding of the Lamb has come, and his bride has made herself ready."

Now, that's a worship service! Who could experience it and not be moved?

Our worship must give the same clarion call. We are the redeemed of the Lord, and we must say so; we enjoy saying so; we get excited saying so; we can't stop saying so.

The Peaceable Kingdom

People in our world are hurting. They long to hear the announcement John heard: "Now the dwelling of God is with men, and he will live with them. They will be his people, and God himself will be with them and be their God. He will wipe every tear from their eyes. There will be no more death or mourning or crying or pain, for the old order of things has passed away."

Can we celebrate the advent of that New Jerusalem in our midst? Its magnitude may be nothing like what John saw, but have we had a taste? Has the kingdom Jesus announced in the Sermon on the Mount come in small measure to us? If it has, the joy of it will be unrestrained in our worship, and the newcomer will notice. It will be a witness.

"The Medium Is the Message"

Back in 1967, in his book by the same name, Marshall McLuhan coined the phrase, "The medium is the message." The way the message is delivered determines (or at least influences) the message that is received. And that concept graphically represents the role worship can have in witnessing to the world. In his book, *Common Roots*, Robert Webber points out that the primary focus of worship is the Lord:

> While evangelism and teaching are integral functions of the church, they should not, as they have in some churches, constitute the sum and substance of worship.... The historic Christian approach to worship which emphasizes the adoration of the Father through the Son has been replaced in some churches by a program with a stage and an audience.[3]

When our priorities and focus in worship are on the Lord, the message of the gospel will be clear. We will seldom have to digress *in that context* to preach a special salvation sermon to the unbelieving visitor. It is a subtle but important difference to be recognized.

Whether through Scripture reading, the affirmation of the Christian creeds, song, preaching, public testimony, confession, prayer, drama, or communion—worship powerfully communicates the gospel *if* . . . *if* it is participatory in nature. If our worship flows out of what we are, what we truly believe, and what we have given our lives to live, it can be extremely powerful.

On the other hand, if it lacks integrity, if it is just something we dutifully do or watch, the unbeliever will detect our sham, and the very action by which we proclaim that Jesus is Lord will deny him.

In this same vein we do well to ask ourselves, are people pointed toward God in our worship, or is attention focused on the cleverness of a few performers?

Unity in the Body

One advantage to the witness quality of worship is that you don't have to beat people over the head with the precepts of the gospel, trying to argue or force their acceptance. In worship, people see what *you* believe. If your life is consistent, you can hardly say it more strongly. George W. Webber wrote:

> Where would one want to take the unconvinced person in order that he might feel the power of the Christian community in depth and reality? Perhaps you would respond that it isn't so simple as all this; you can't expect someone to come into a church and in one or two visits find the depth of true community that exists. I'm not so sure, however, that in the house churches of the first century the pagan was not confronted with a startling awareness that something here was different. Was it not precisely the power of the early church that men and women, living in the Roman world, saw that in the church wealthy women, slaves, and soldiers came together in Christian love and oneness? This was so shattering a miracle that the world had to take it seriously. As was said then, "Look at those Christians; see how they love one another." The world is always astonished when diversity is overcome by oneness. This is the miracle of the Christian fellowship.[4]

This is also our challenge. *Does* the world experience unity among us? Or do we confuse unity with being all alike? Does the visitor to our church think, "I'm not like the people here; I'm sure I would not fit in. I guess Christianity is not for me"? Or does the visitor think, "There are many types of people here, and all seem to love one another in spite of their differences in age or dress or color. Yes, I would probably be welcome here, too"? It is unity even amidst diversity that is the real miracle in our lives.

The media has a heyday when Christian groups fight with one another. Denominations split, "conservatives," "moderates," and "liberals" take sides, televangelists point fingers at other televangelists—and the name of Christ is mocked. Not many are saying in our time, "Look at those Christians; see how they love one another." Not many are in awe of *God* when we are at worship.

Unity among Christians should be a concern for all those who witness in Christ's name. And we must begin with our own congregations. We must remember that "church" is not a place we go to, but who we are: the family of God. Our worship services must be a place we can bring those to whom we are witnessing, and say, "Come and see what God has done."

For Group Discussion

1. How might a worship service convict a person of sin even when sin is not the subject of the service?

2. In ancient times monarchs demanded obeisance and even worship. Whether the monarchs deserved it or not, this practice provided people with an experience of worshiping someone as "greater" than themselves. Can you think of any ways in modern society that we genuinely learn to consider anyone greater than ourselves? How might that affect our ability and freedom to worship God?

3. Discuss the issue of preserving dignity in the context of worship. Who is being served and to what end?

4. How is the medium the message in terms of our worship and witness?

5. This chapter identifies several fundamentals that should be evident in our worship. What other truths might we hope would also come through?

CHAPTER SEVEN

How to Close the Back Door

"Where have the MacKennas been?" Helen asked in the elders meeting.

"Well, they were coming regularly, but I guess I haven't seen them for several weeks," admitted the pastor.

"John hasn't been to men's breakfast the last couple months, either," said Roger.

No one seemed to know what had happened to the MacKennas.. They had moved into town last summer and had started attending church with real gratefulness for the friendly contact from the evangelism team. But now they had fallen between the cracks.

According to James C. Bland, pastor of Kendall Presbyterian Church in Miami, Florida, "Assimilation of new members is often the missing link between successful evangelism and faithful shepherding."[4] It's the disastrous syndrome of the *open back door* out which newcomers too often walk.

What's worse, when those people are contacted a second time, they are less inclined to give the church a try. Why should they? They've already tasted and not been satisfied.

What was missing?

Friendship and Purpose

James Bland conducted a survey and came up with what he believes is a solution. "In the past, our quarterly new-members classes emphasized our church history, doctrine, and practice of the sacraments. Now, the primary purpose has become helping new members build friendships and assume an active role."[2]

Long before Bland's research, Ray Stedman, of the Peninsula Bible Church in Palo Alto, California, experimented with a major restructuring of his large congregation to achieve these ends. His "Body Life" services emphasized sharing and mutual support characteristic of the early church's *koininia.*

Periodically the church seems to go through cycles of forgetting and then rediscovering this most powerful quality. Stedman says:

> What we call the church is really two churches. Both are religious but one is selfish, power-hungry, cruel and devilish. The other is strong, loving, forgiving and godly. One has fomented human hatred and caused society to erupt in continual bloody conflicts, all done in the name of God and religion. The other has healed human hurt, broken down barriers of race and class and delivered men and women everywhere from fear, guilt, shame and ignorance.[3]

In his book, *Body Life,* Stedman then set out—largely through a study of Ephesians—how church members can fulfill the function of edifying one another in love.

Solid Research

However, since Stedman's work, much more study has been done on the dynamics of church growth—what helps people come into the church and what keeps them there as active, ministering members of the body of Christ.

In 1965 Donald McGavran, broadly recognized as the dean of the modern Church Growth Movement, started the Fuller School of World Mission and Institute of Church Growth at Fuller Seminary in Pasadena, California. Since then his solid research has been aided and disseminated by such colleagues as

Win Arn, Lyle E. Schaller, John Wimber, and C. Peter Wagner.

The Church Growth Movement has been criticized by such notables as John Howard Yoder and Howard Snyder for its temptation to "spiritual technology." Yet the movement's scientific research has provided us with useful ways of incorporating new persons into the church. Failure to heed the research may perpetuate barriers that keep people from Christ.

Some Numbers Do Count

Church growth experts do look at numbers, but they recognize that numbers do not tell the whole story of a church's health. Peter Wagner says,

> I am not interested in names on church rolls. There are already too many nominal, inactive and nonresident church members in America. I am not interested in churches which are religious social clubs. I am not interested in decisions for Christ totaled up as people raise their hands or come forward after a crusade. I am not interested in Christians who profess faith in Christ but do not demonstrate it in their lives. These numbers are unimportant. . . .
>
> I am interested in responsible church members   who continue "steadfastly in the apostles' doctrine and fellowship, and in breaking of bread, and in prayers" (Acts 2:42) as did believers in the Jerusalem church.[4]

Several years ago Campus Crusade's *Here's Life* campaign produced impressive numbers of conversions. But in studying the reports from a dozen American cities, Roland E. Griswold, founder of the Office of Church Expansion for the Advent Christian denomination, discovered that only three percent of those who received Christ as a result of the campaign found their way onto any church membership rolls. And of those, 42 percent were already members of some other church.[5] Certainly numbers must be qualified before they help us see what really works and what doesn't.

But some numbers do count. A church that is not growing (in terms of converting new people to Christ as committed disciples) is dying. To merely keep pace with the world's expanding population the church must grow, to say nothing of fulfilling Christ's great commission.

The Barrier of Size

What are some of the factors that welcome people into a church and keep the back door closed so they don't wander on out? What makes people feel sufficiently included and needed to stay and give their lives to Jesus?

According to Lyle Schaller, the attendance of half the churches in America is 75 or less for Sunday morning worship, and only 5 percent average over 350.[6] There are identifiable reasons why many churches experience various size barriers. No matter how hard they work, they can't seem to permanently include more people. It's as though the back door opens to relieve the pressure when new people come in. And most often those who end up leaving are the ones that just came in.

One such barrier is the maximum number of members a single pastor can minister to personally—know everyone's names, visit each home periodically, call when a member is sick, do basic counseling, perform baptisms, weddings, and funerals, and relate to the church as a family. Wagner says that this relationship can be maintained with as many as 200 members, occasionally a few more. "But in order to get through the 200 barrier and sustain a healthy rate of growth, the pastor must be willing to pay a price too high for some: he or she must be willing to shift from a *shepherd* to a *rancher* mode."[7] The rancher is a manager who is willing to delegate the task of one-on-one shepherding to other leaders in the church.

This is how members of Robert Schuller's 10,000 member Crystal Cathedral can consistently declare it to be the friend-

liest church in Orange County. His associate has intensively
trained some 700 lay ministers for pastoral care.[7]

You may not have a desire to see your church grow to that
size, but don't forget that the model church in Jerusalem incor-
porated about 3,000 new people in a single day (Acts 2:41).
With most of our churches averaging no more than a hundred,
we need to raise our sights and break a few barriers.

Ways to Break the Size Barrier

There are ways to successfully break those barriers without
sacrificing intimacy and responsible discipleship. Wagner suggests the following organizational formula:

Celebration + Congregation + Cell = Church[9]

The Celebration

Wagner claims that celebration—what most people mean by
corporate Sunday morning worship—is not inhibited by large
size. In many ways it is enhanced by numbers. It begins to give
us a vision of the *people of God*, the great cloud of witnesses
that have gone before or gather elsewhere in the world. It gives
us a glimpse of God's majesty, and we can release ourselves to
his movement.

Indeed, when numbers are too few, this kind of worship is
often stifled. The singing is not robust. The worship is dull.
There is little that is festive or victorious.

But, you may say, celebration can be impersonal. It can lack
the very *koinonia* we are wanting to foster to help people feel
involved. True. That's why there's more.

The Congregation

Congregation is the ceiling that limits growth in most
churches. It is the maximum number of people that allows

face-to-face relationships—with everyone knowing everyone else by name. They know where they live, what they do, the kids' names, and when they are on vacation. It incorporates the clan or small-town feel. Wagner used to think the maximum size for a congregation was about 250. But more recently, he has reduced the ideal size for a congregation to between 30 and 80.

Of course, the numbers can float on up toward that 200 figure and still work. But the barrier begins to be felt when there are new persons for three or four Sundays and you still don't know their names.

Reba Place Church in Evanston, Illinois, exceeded the size barrier for the "congregation" substantially during the late '70s. But to do so they employed some exceptional methods to keep up with one another. They lived communally in 15 large extended-family households all within a four block neighborhood. They shared a common purse and corporate decision making. They spent over six hours a week in large group meetings for adults, plus another dozen hours together in smaller groupings. Even then, when the size exceeded 300 adults and children, their openness to new people unintentionally began to break down. In spite of the great number of hours invested in life together, some members began to feel removed from the decision-making process. The congregation was too cumbersome and unresponsive for each one to own it. The fact that the church was divided into small groups (or "cells" as Wagner calls them) was not enough. Everyone was still trying to embrace the whole.

Now, as a church, they have broken into five "clusters," or smaller congregations. Each of these requires a much less intensive schedule, and three are noncommunal. "We've learned not to worry if we don't know all about someone in another cluster because we do know the people in our own cluster, and we know that other people are looking out for that person in the other cluster," says one satisfied member. "And now we are emotionally much more free to welcome new people."

The Cell

Cell groups are another critical element in the design of a church that is trying to eliminate barriers to receiving new people. If the congregation is the face-to-face encounter in church, the cell is the heart-to-heart experience. In these small groups, each person knows and is known, and all are cared for like family.

Much more will be said about small groups (chapters 9 and 10), but Wagner points out that they may not be for everyone:

> Some people in rural areas where their extended family lives in close proximity, for example, are not usually inclined toward participation in small church groups. . . . Some with a low level of verbal skills feel very uncomfortable in a cell group where spiritual intimacy and accountability is developed. Exceptions should be made for such people, and they should not be allowed to develop guilt complexes if they are not socially or psychologically adaptable to small groups.[10]

Birds of a Feather . . . .

One other finding of church growth research is that the *homogeneous factor* plays a major role in whether people want to stay once they come through the front door. This is one of the most broadly criticized principles of the Church Growth Movement. Essentially it says that people like to be with their own kind and will feel comfortable in a church where they can do so. On the other hand, they'll drift away from any church where they are forced to sacrifice their cultural distinctives.

But somehow most of us don't feel it is right to encourage that tendency.

The love Christians have for one another is a powerful witness. Jesus said, "By this all men will know that you are my disciples, if you love one another" (John 13:35). But, "If you love those who love you, what credit is that to you? Even 'sinners' love those who love them" (Luke 6:32). He implied—in the context of church growth—that there is no unique "witness power" in encouraging birds of a feather to flock together.

Nonetheless, say the church growth experts, that's the way people respond, and we must deal with that tendency if we are going to introduce them to Christ. Wagner suggests that some of the notable congregations that *seem* to demonstrate cross-cultural vitality merely represent churches made up of similar-minded, cause-oriented, politically liberal intellectuals—a subgroup in their own right where the average farmer or factory worker or beautician would feel so uncomfortable they would choke . . . and vice versa.

Wagner points to Circle Church in Chicago as an example of how homogeneous an apparently mixed church can be:

> Circle Church would be even less likely than mine to get an unconverted Archie Bunker to consider the claims of Jesus Christ. All he would need to make him look for the door would be one look at the blacks, the far-out dress, the elitist, liberal books on the booktable, the *Sojourners* and *The Other Side* for sale in the magazine rack, the dashikis, the long hair, and men wearing beards. Then if he heard the soul choir, the heavy social implications of the sermon (which he would probably interpret as "pinko"), the abstract level of conversation in the corridors, and the avant-garde worship format, he would disappear once and for all.[11]

Circle Church thrived in this style during the late '60s and early '70s when integration was chic and people felt a lot of guilt over the fact that "eleven o'clock Sunday morning is the most segregated hour in America." But when black cultural consciousness began to rise, some of Circle's blacks no longer thought it was so cool to watch whites acting funky, and they began to worry that they might be losing a little too much of their own soul. Ultimately, as a group, they left Circle to start their own church.

Cautious Flocking Together

We naturally fear that which is strange. But if we don't mix, we can't understand, and others will seem to remain strange and frightening to us. Before long we will become active participants in discrimination. We won't want to live near people who are *too* different, send our children to school with them, or work with them. And we certainly will hesitate to entrust them with power and authority in business and civic affairs.

Courageous Christians were on the forefront of the Civil Rights Movement. Unfortunately, fearful Christians stood on the other sides of the picket lines vigorously and brutally trying to perpetuate discrimination and mandatory segregation.

So what can we do to preserve the rich components of various cultures (if there is no biblical discord) while fostering the kind of understanding and love that can only come through familiarity between peoples?

Here are some possible considerations:

- Understanding, sensitivity, and respect between groups is far more important than aping another culture's distinctives or scolding those who don't enjoy them.
- Cross-cultural contact should begin at the leadership level—pastor to pastor, executive to executive, lay leader to lay leader. This is because the leaders should be the most mature and secure people, meriting mutual respect and diminishing patterns of condescension or deference when they interact.
- We should not expect extensive cross-cultural interaction from non-Christians or new Christians when that represents a burden or threat to them.
- Within the same church, "congregations" or "cells" focused toward subgroups can help preserve cultural distinctives while fostering mutual respect and love.

• If inroads into a new group are to be attempted, some means for allowing the new people to remain with their own kind—at least for a while—will be needed.

These approaches seem obvious to us when we are trying to bridge groups that aren't distinguished by race, culture, or class (where we are so often driven by guilt). For instance, if a church of predominantly older members decided to reach out to university students on a nearby campus, they would not expect the young people to find their company very exciting. They would know enough to create a young people's group and possibly hire a youth minister. That doesn't mean that the two groups have nothing to offer each other, but to be comfortable, they also need a way to gather separately where more is shared in common.

Creative Inclusion

Uptown Baptist Church in Chicago is a good example of a church's wise acknowledgment that some differences between people have a value worth preserving. In mid-1980 Uptown Baptist sponsored three Cambodian refugee families and shortly thereafter became heavily involved with other Cambodian refugees settling in their neighborhood.

At first the church simply tried to incorporate the Cambodians in the American service. But, even though most of the Cambodians were eager to learn English, it became clear in less than a year that they needed something of their own. An American service done in the Khmer language was not even adequate. It was ultimately necessary to establish an authentically Cambodian service. Now the Cambodian congregation (of 50 adult members) has its own leadership and full-time pastor.

Consider the rich cross-cultural sharing that is represented by the following report from some Anglos with whom the

Cambodians from Uptown Baptist Church shared a recent Easter celebration.

> We sat enthralled as the cast of Cambodians put on an Easter drama. The dialogue was in the Khmer language, but the story was biblically faithful and easy to follow. What struck us most was the intensity of the characters.
>
> When the soldiers dragged Jesus before Pilate, they marched, yelling: "Hup! Hup! Hup!" with every other step. A chill ran down our spines. How many of them had witnessed soldiers dragging a friend or relative away?
>
> Then came a moment when the soldiers dumped the lifeless body of Jesus at the feet of Joseph of Arimathea. Hol Pav (Joseph) reverently crossed the hands of Kounasith Keo (Jesus) across his chest. There was blood on his hands and feet. Three women—Bun Sing, Kheng Choy, and Jodi Sutimek—knelt by the body and gently began washing his face and wiping the blood from his hands and feet. Tears poured down our faces. How many times had these very Cambodians tenderly washed the bodies of their own dead?[12]

It hardly would have meant the same with a mixed cast. And yet the opportunity for sharing the drama resulted from multiple congregations functioning under the umbrella of the same church.

People come and stay in a church when they are fully received, engaged with genuine friendship, allowed to serve, and helped to feel at home.

For Group Discussion

1. Would you consider your pastor a "rancher" or a "shepherd"? If your pastor were to change, what would it cost you? Your pastor? The whole church?

2. What might it mean to say that "if the church is not growing, it is dying"? Can you think of any legitimate reason why a church can't grow? (There are some.)

3. If Peter Wagner's formula, "Celebration + Congregation + Cell = Church," is accurate, what components are represented in your church? What are the sizes of those components?

4. What are the "birds of a feather" that characterize your church? How do you feel about that arrangement?

Witness: Community

In community persons enter into and are nourished by relationships through which transformation into Christlikeness occurs. This may include one-on-one or small group or family relationships as well as school settings or large groups. As persons learn to trust, forgive, receive counsel, and care for others, the discipling community takes on the character of Jesus.

CHAPTER EIGHT

Witness Rooted in Discipleship

Fewer and fewer people were participating in the midweek meeting of North Main Street Mennonite Church in Nappanee, Indiana. So Sunday school teacher Don Miller suggested to his class that they meet for Bible study on Wednesday night as a way to facilitate deeper fellowship.

Twenty people signed up at first. But as Don was trying to decide what to study, he became aware of the book, *The Master's Plan* by Win Arn, complete with a kit and video for training others to reach out. He proposed that the group study this, instead, as the first step in a discipleship process. But as people realized the degree of commitment required, the resulting group dropped to six persons.

"At first I was worried," admits Don. "The six who signed up were not leadership types at all, just ordinary church members. But as we got into the study, I realized this was the perfect group. The whole point of discipling is to train every Christian to in turn reach out and train others to spread the gospel."

Like a pebble dropped in a pond, the ripples are already beginning to widen. The study group has recently completed the training program, and they plan to go into already existing groups in the church (youth group, Sunday school classes, etc.) and take people who want to through the training program. "Our goal," explains Don, "is to train a core of people, who will train others in the church, who will then reach out to their 'extended family'—friends, neighbors, relatives."

This group of six (seven including Don) has also sponsored three social events at the church in which each person that came had to bring another person from their work or neighborhood with them. The purpose was not to get these people to come to church per se, but just to spend time with a group of Christians.

Byron Yoder, a member of the group, says, "This is not a program, but a *process*. A program has a beginning and an end. The Master's Plan has no end, just a beginning. Our whole purpose is to win souls for Christ. We aren't out to play the numbers game; we're out to love people and let them know Christ loves them."

Byron also admits, "Sometimes I feel a bit scared with what we are trying to accomplish. We have some very big goals, but we also have a very big God."

Look at Your Present Group

Like Don and Byron, you probably already belong to at least one small Christian group, perhaps more. Many church members attend a Sunday school class. In addition, many participate in service activities, young adult fellowships, prayer breakfasts, or parenting groups. Others may meet voluntarily in small groups for discussion, Bible study, or prayer.

Before you dash off to be a Lone Ranger soul-winner, or form a new evangelism team, it's important to assess your present involvements within the body of Christ. Ask yourself: Do the groups to which you already belong have evangelistic power? Would an unsaved person coming into your fellowship (of whatever type—Sunday school class, prayer breakfast, support group) feel drawn to Christ? Would he or she discover there a quality of life not known elsewhere? If Christ is truly the center of your fellowship *and your relationships within the group*, the answer should be a positive *yes*. It is as certainly *no* if your group is merely a social gathering where members are bound together by secular interests, or merely discusses religious issues without personal application.

Unless yours is an unusual group, some would have to admit, if they were absolutely honest, that moneymaking interests them more than soul-winning. Your group is even more exceptional if it has no members who deny the love of Christ by gossip, faultfinding, or superior attitudes toward others. Probably there are some whose practice of Christian discipleship has been weakened by love of comfort or of beautiful things. Though you love all of them, in spite of their shortcomings, you'd be the first to admit that your group is not totally under the control of Christ.

Pull Out or Stay Put?

What can you do about this situation? There is, of course, the possibility of pulling out and starting a new group composed only of those who are totally committed to full obedience as you understand it. Many Christians report that new life has been born in churches through the formation of small groups committed to know and to do the will of God more perfectly and faithfully.

However, most of our congregations already have such a full schedule of church-related activities that merely to think about one more meeting to attend makes us tired. "Christians will find themselves distracted and their home life further weakened if they attempt to be loyal to the existing calendar of essential church activities, and then in addition set up another series of gatherings of cell, prayer, or search-for-renewal groups," wrote Paul M. Miller.[1]

If adding more groups is not always the answer, abandoning the old ones has its price:

The average congregation is not so dead or corrupt that it is time for [people] seeking God's highest to withdraw their most vital interest and support from the existing prayer meetings and Sunday school classes. The average pastor is not so closed to God's renewing work in the church that he needs to be left high and dry with the deadwood of the membership and the calendar of activities while those who desire God's highest set up other activities as rivals for the faithful worker's time.[2]

As we respond to God's call to be witnesses, it is important to consider whether God wants to use us to build each other up for service right where we are, within the relationships and groups we have already. But whether forming new groups or renewing existing ones, there are some important things to consider that are foundational to preparing yourself, your group, and your local church body as witnesses.

Beware of Spiritual Elitism

The twelve whom Jesus called to be with him and to preach the gospel prove that God can work through a group composed of imperfect persons. Not a single one of the original disciples had the spiritual maturity that would make him a desirable member of a spiritually elite circle. Even after nearly three years under Christ's influence, the chosen ones displayed vengefulness, covetousness, boastfulness, and infidelity. Yet, as he used these persons, Christ transformed them. An exclusive group contradicts the nature of Christian fellowship, which is reconciling and inclusive, uniting within itself men and women of all types and from varying backgrounds.

Reflecting on his experience with the study group at North Main Street, Byron Yoder said, "One thing I'm realizing is how God works through ordinary people. The seven of us in the original study group call ourselves 'God's Clods.' We're learning that God uses ordinary people who aren't perfect to accomplish his will and purposes. The disciples of Jesus were God's

Clods. Abraham was one of God's Clods. God's power shows up best in weakness. God's going to do great things at North Main Street if people will only depend on him and not themselves."

This does not mean that there isn't value in coming together with those who feel a similar call from God upon their lives for a particular task or mission. Several men and women at Reba Place Church, in Evanston, Illinois, have recently formed an Urban Mission Group to explore their mutual leanings toward urban ministry. Each one left a previous small group in order to focus more of their time and energy in this direction. The direction of the group is not yet clear, but they came together to get to know one another more deeply and seek the Lord for guidance.

But as most of us know, even groups with a common task or mission are made up of people of widely varying temperaments, experiences, backgrounds, personalities. Learning to live and work in love with the imperfect members of your group is good training for evangelism. It's important to ask ourselves, "If we can't love each other, how can we love the world?"

Begin Where You Are

An effective evangelistic program, however, does not depend on waiting until your group is fully prepared for the work of evangelism. Renewal in Christian life and evangelism are so closely connected that one cannot occur without the other. Facing the fact that many church members are unprepared to witness, Tom Allan wrote:

> The only way to prepare a church for evangelism is by the work of evangelism. . . . It is a mistake to say that we must cleanse the inner life of our church before we undertake the work of evangelism, and

>strengthen the faithful before we set about reclaiming the lapsed or challenging the careless. *The faithful can be strengthened insofar as they are going out to the lapsed and the careless* [italics added].[3]

Those who wait for a perfect group of Christians before they begin fellowship evangelism will never begin. All Christian groups must start where they are, believing in the power of God to use unfit instruments and to fit them in the using for greater service. Even the most mature Christian cannot profess to be superior to unbelievers, a perfect model of Christianity for them to follow.

If your group can honestly admit to one another and to those whom you desire to win that you, too, are sinners in constant need of forgiveness, you can begin to evangelize.

How Evangelism Begins

What can you do to get your group started in evangelism? Groups are apt, when thinking about renewed evangelistic effort, to consider first some plan for interesting, enlisting, or organizing members to do the work. A plan may indeed be valuable in helping those who are already concerned to see what to do and how to do it. Before adopting any plan, however, we must be aware that even the most carefully worked out organization is only a tool. Any approach which considers only organization and strategy carries the seeds of failure.

Witness and service bear fruit only as they flow spontaneously from hearts filled with the love of Christ which expresses itself in concern for others. Such love is evident by the power of the Holy Spirit. The witness of the first-century church did not grow out of any carefully structured evangelistic organization. Men and women living in obedience to the Holy Spirit worked and witnessed at the Spirit's direction and through the Spirit's power. Only the Holy Spirit can revitalize the witness and service of the twentieth century.

What You Can Do

Though you cannot do the work of the Holy Spirit, you can help to create the conditions in which the Spirit can work. If you feel that the small group to which you belong is not sufficiently Spirit-directed to be a power for evangelism, you can put yourself at the Spirit's disposal to be used according to the Spirit's will. Consider the following as first steps in preparing your group for evangelism.

Accept Your Responsibility

The Spirit of God dwells in your group through you and through the other members individually. Thus the responsibility of bringing your fellowship more fully under the Spirit's guidance begins with you. As you place your life more fully under God's direction, the Spirit will have moved into a more central position in your circle. A fellowship becomes Spirit-controlled *as individual members yield to the Spirit*, not by any show-of-hands vote deciding to allow the Spirit to lead.

Let the Spirit Work in You

In any meeting of your group, whenever you feel that Christ is not being given his rightful place, immediately ask him to take his rightful place in you. Reexamine the contribution you have made to the group. Has everything you have said or done been at the Spirit's direction? Allow his Spirit to check your attitudes, your feelings toward others, your secret thoughts. It may well be that you will become so busy repenting of your own sins and setting your own heart in order that you will have no time left to bewail the spiritual lack of your friends.

Examine Your Own Discipleship

Likewise, before you find fault with the quality of discipleship practiced by others, take a hard look at your own commitment to Christ:

- Have you really, as far as you know, surrendered completely to him . . . or do you feel threatened to give up control of your life?
- Are you seeking to know and to do his will in the situations you meet each day . . . or do you act out of habit? Does he have first claim on your time . . . or are you too busy to spend time in personal prayer?
- Are your possessions his to use as he chooses . . . or are you reluctant to share your lawn mower or loan your car?
- Do you do your daily work as service for him . . . or do you complain regularly?
- Are you showing his love by your actions and attitudes toward the people you live and work with every day . . . or is it easier to love "the lost" than it is to love your family or co-workers?
- Do you welcome opportunities to use your talents for his service . . . or are you most concerned with "self-fulfillment"?
- Does your life bear witness to the reality of the faith you profess . . . or would your neighbors be surprised to learn you are a Christian?
- Are you willing to be shown the faults and sins which hinder your witness . . . or do you feel defensive when someone gently corrects you?
- Do you have the courage to confess and forsake your sins . . . or do you indulge your weaknesses in private?
- Does your own devotional life have the reality you would like to see in the experience of others . . . or are you putting on a spiritual front?
- Does God actually speak to you through the Word . . . or do you have a hard time concentrating on the same old verses?
- Are you consciously communing with God as you pray . . . or does your mind wander?
- Do you truly meet God when you participate in group worship services . . . or are you there from habit and a sense of spiritual duty?
- Is Christ a living, ever-present friend to you . . . or is your testimony always a rerun of "when I got saved"?

Check the Clarity of Your Witness

In the same way, before you grieve that your group is inarticulate or uncertain in its spoken witness, check on the clarity of your own testimony for Christ. Can you tell in words what he means to you? Can you explain how you came to know him?

In a group of suggestions designed to help pastors encourage their members to witness for Christ, Nelson E. Kauffman included a list of questions to stimulate personal testimony. While intended primarily for group discussion, they are printed here to help you personally review your own spiritual pilgrimage.

1. What were the factors in your life, such as people, services, sermons, friends, experiences of sickness, and fear, which led you to see yourself as a sinner condemned before God and in need of Christ?

2. What experiences in your life led you finally to make the decision to receive Christ as your Savior? What struggles did you go through before you finally made up your mind? Describe your struggles and how you overcame them.

3. What were the things (such as the Scriptures and personal experiences) which helped you understand *how* to receive Christ as your Savior, and really accept his forgiveness? How long did you attend church before you were able to trust him and have assurance of that forgiveness? How do you know your position in Christ?

4. What in your experience helped you make the Bible and God's promises effective in your life, to the extent that you can help others to apply God's promises to their experiences?

5. How and from whom, or from what, did you receive most or much spiritual help in your early Christian experience?

6. What things gave you the most trouble or caused you the most problems as you attempted to make spiritual progress?

7. What gives you confidence in your salvation, your peace and joy in Christ, which you would recommend to others?

8. Is Christianity relevant to your everyday life? How?

9. What are some of the things you appreciate and are thankful for in the church to which you belong and which make you feel like inviting others to Christ and to fellowship in your church?

10. What experiences of giving your testimony for Christ have you had that have been a real blessing, joy, and help to you?

11. Have you ever been led by the Spirit to do some personal witnessing, which you did, or which you failed to do, and what were the forces, fears, or strengthening factors which affected your decision?

12. What kind of help do you feel you and your fellow church members need in order to become more effective personal witnesses for Christ?

13. What are the things that you feel do most to keep us from speaking to others about faith and salvation in Christ?

14. How would you explain salvation to one who asked you how to be saved? Present each step carefully.

Study

Besides being ready to give your personal testimony for Christ in words, you need—if your group is to have a clear witness—to be well informed on the biblical basis of your faith. This means serious Bible study and familiarity with the doctrines of your church.

Also, if you are to serve effectively in the world, you need to know what's going on in the world. Keeping up-to-date on world news is your Christian duty. Many sincere Christians fail in their witness because they are totally unable to relate the gospel message to the needs of modern men and women. Usually this is not because they themselves have not found Christ satisfying, but because they don't know enough of what's happening outside of their immediate circles to understand what other people think and talk about, what they fear, or what they want most from life.

Practice Neglected Principles

Above all, you can help to prepare your group for evangelism by personally putting into practice Christian principles of group relationships. The best manual for the study of wholesome group dynamics is the New Testament. The biblical teaching about Christian love and its practical applications is much talked about. Several principles, however, are often overlooked, such as the following:

• *Take an interest in ordinary people.* "Take a real interest in ordinary people," is Phillips' translation of Romans 12:16b. Christians should be interested in people because of who they are or what they can become, not because of their title or what they can do for us. But instead of building friendship with the lonely persons who would be cheered by expressions of love, we flood popular persons with attention.

Taking a real interest in ordinary people demands unselfishness. It is so much more fun to tag along with the leader who entertains with lively conversation, charms with attractive ways, or challenges by spiritual acumen. Christian love, however, does not lead us to seek satisfaction for our own ego or relief for our loneliness. Like the love of Christ, it seeks to give rather than to receive.

• *Develop a readiness to forgive and ask forgiveness.* We should approach our brothers and sisters in Christ with a readiness to forgive their weaknesses. One who really forgives cannot cherish a secret contempt for the sinner. Forgiveness grows out of sincere humility toward God and others. We will find it easier to be charitable toward our failing brother and sister when we honestly face Jesus' question, "Why do you look at the speck of sawdust in your brother's eye and pay no attention to the plank in your own eye?" (Matt. 7:3).

Every opportunity to forgive another can be a reminder of our own need to be forgiven. Bonhoeffer wrote:

> Even when sin and misunderstanding burden the communal life, is not the sinning brother still a brother, with whom I, too, stand under the Word of Christ? Will not his sin be a constant occasion for me to give thanks that both of us may live in the forgiving love of God in Jesus Christ? Thus the very hour of disillusionment with my brother becomes incomparably salutary, because it so thoroughly teaches me that neither of us can ever live by our own words and deeds, but only by that one Word and Deed which really binds us together—the forgiveness of sins in Jesus Christ.[4]

At the same time, it is very important to keep things clear between ourselves and others. If a brother sins against me, or I see a sister in sin, it is my responsibility to go to him or her personally, in a humble and loving spirit, not to judge but for the purpose of restoring the relationship (Matt. 18:15-17). If I sense that I have hurt or sinned against a brother or sister, I need to make asking forgiveness and restoring the relationship a priority before I return to my worship and service for the Lord (Matt. 5:23-24). We need to avoid the extremes of brushing things under the rug to keep from making waves, or rushing to judgment over every hurt feeling.

• *Keep a sober estimate of yourself.* "In humility consider others better than yourselves," wrote Paul in Philippians 2:3. At another time he advised, "I say to every one of you: Do not think of yourself more highly than you ought" (Rom. 12:3). Those who remember these two admonitions cannot be headstrong when they exchange ideas.

A Christian who has a sober estimate of herself will not try to force her own opinions on someone else. A person who esteems others better than himself will allow them freedom to speak and will listen to their suggestions with respect, admitting that their ideas may be better than his own. It is quite presumptuous, really, for anyone to assume that the Holy Spirit has revealed to him and only to him all of God's truth. Christ's promise, "When he, the Spirit of truth, comes, he will guide you into all truth" (John 16:13), was spoken not to an individual but to the disciples as a group. When Christ's followers humbly share with one another the fragments of truth revealed by the Spirit to each one, together under the Spirit's guidance they will arrive at fuller truth.

• *Have faith in others.* To learn from one another, Christians need to trust one another. Even in small groups, Christians tend to lack confidence in other Christians. You might protest, "How can I trust Henry who doesn't open his Bible from one Sunday to the next? Or Ethel, whose life advertises worldliness? Or self-righteous Richard, with all his moralism and dogmatism? Or wishy-washy Kitty, whose thinking echoes that of the last person she talked to? Or Arthur, who leans toward too liberal a theology? I'll try to love and help them, but don't ask me to have faith in them."

Is your group less trustworthy than the church at Corinth? Read again Paul's first letter to them. Notice all the evidences of their immaturity and lack of spirituality. Yet Paul wrote:

> I always thank God for you because of his grace given you in Christ Jesus. For in him you have been enriched in every way—in all your speaking and in all your knowledge—because our testimony about Christ was confirmed in you. Therefore you do not lack any spiritual gift as you eagerly wait for our Lord Jesus Christ to be revealed. He will keep you strong to the end, so that you will be blameless on the day of our Lord Jesus Christ (1 Cor. 1:4-8).

The secret of Paul's confidence is found in the next verse, "God . . . is faithful." Paul's trust was in what God would do through the Corinthians. You, too, can have faith in your group because your faith is not in the other persons but in what God will do through them. Just as in your own relationship with God you exercise faith, not in yourself, but in the power of Christ in you, so you can have confidence in other Christians. To love another person as yourself means showing that person the same tolerance you show yourself. You know you are not perfect. You recognize your failures and sins. Yet you trust God to forgive, cleanse, and fit you for service. Can you not trust him to do the same for your brothers and sisters in Christ?

• *Seek out fellowship.* As you practice confidence in other Christians, you will find them responding to it. Faith has creative power. Stephen Boyd, a Southern Baptist pastor and college professor, maintains, "We empower people by needing them." Ask God to guide you to others in your group with whom you can share your concern that your fellowship grow in its witness. Like Elijah, you will probably find that you do not stand alone. Likely others have been waiting for someone to lead in this new direction. Together you can agree to prepare yourself by Bible study, by cultivating a regular devotional life, and by seeking to let the Holy Spirit work freely with you.

God Uses Imperfect Groups

If you are willing to be honest before the Lord about your own discipleship and put into practice principles of group relationships, God can use your group even though it is not a perfect group.

The leader of a voluntary service unit, in which members experienced a very real work of the Spirit both in personal renewal and in evangelistic power, gave this testimony:

There are always those who sit on the fringes of fellowship or who perhaps even harden themselves spiritually although still present physically because of the structure of the situation. Such persons are not a hindrance, however, but rather a blessing to the group; for they continually present to the group the challenge to love and enfold and in a sense give the group a feeling of incompleteness which forces it to throw itself on the Lord even more completely for his cleansing and grace. In other words, I believe that Christ comes and makes himself seen in every broken heart, and unbroken hearts only serve to make his presence more definite, for the contrast is so amazing. This means that if the Lord is not moving in a group, it is not because the group is not altogether pure, but because, search as he will, the Lord cannot find a single broken heart in which to begin his work of love.

For Group Discussion

1. List the small groups in which you currently participate. List other groups in your church.

2. Take a hard look at your own commitment to Christ by answering the questions under the heading, "Examine Your Own Discipleship."

3. In the same way, before you grieve that your group is inarticulate or uncertain in its spoken witness, "Check the Clarity of Your Witness" for Christ by going over the questions from the section by the same name.

4. Identify one of the commonly neglected principles that you should work on and discuss it with others.

CHAPTER NINE

Witness Through Christian Fellowship

The fellowship of a Spirit-directed small group strengthens each member for individual witness. After two years as part of a close-knit voluntary service unit, one VSer testified,

> I can't explain what happened to me these two years while in VS. All I know is that I'm different. I look at life, people, work, everything differently. Christ makes sense to me now in a way he never did before this experience. I guess what happened is that I have learned to know Christ in a more personal way than I thought was possible before. Witnessing for him is a very joyful experience now.[1]

The VSer had experienced the benefits of a small group.

The Nature of Small Groups

But before you set out to form new small groups in your church, take time to identify those that already exist and recognize the diversity that they represent. There are many types of small groups that often go unlabled as "a small group": midweek prayer meeting, Sunday school class, or choir, for example. Of course, the degree that they provide a means of receiving new people may be small.

A careful review of the chart on the next page will help highlight many of the variables between groups, including some of their respective strengths and weaknesses.

TYPES OF SMALL GROUPS

	Purpose	Traits	Required	Comments
Task Group	Complete specific project	a—3 b—1 c—1 d—2	Ability, maturity, and commitment to acomplish the task	Provides a way to contribute and be involved in church life, a "role"
Prayer Group	Pray for group members' needs and others outside the group	a—4 b—3 c—2 d—2	To usually attend and to have real concern for others	Can be monopolized by some people but offers love support to newcomers
Bible Study Group	Learn what the Bible says	a—5 b—2 c—2 d—3	Regular participation and usually some homework	Good for neighborhood outreach and evangelism, also for Sunday school
House Church Group	Worship, learn, minister, grow, in an intimate setting	a—4 b—3 c—3 d—5	Frequent attendance, active participation in worship, sharing	Can undermine whole church by duplication if ill-managed, but is inclusive
Fellowship Group	Develop relationships and caring support	a—2 b—4 c—3 d—4	Regular participation and a willingness to share	Low-key version of covenant group, can incorporate prayer and Bible study
Covenant Group	Discipleship, commitment, accountability, support	a—1 b—5 c—5 d—5	Always attend, openness and honesty, desire to be accountable	Can become too internally focused and harsh but has great maturing potential

"Traits" are graded 1-5, 5 being high
  a—Potential for incorporating new people
  b—Degree of relationship among members
  c—Pastoral care provided
  d—Training needed by leader

Any specific group may represent significant crossover between the types described. For instance, a fellowship group may incorporate the characteristics of a task group when it decides to visit all the new people who move into town during the year. (It is usually possible to get a list of new residents from utility companies or city hall.)

Roles to Be Fulfilled in a Group

To get an overview of small-group dynamics, it is helpful to envision how people function in small groups. In his book, *Getting Together*,[2] Em Griffin identifies several roles that people play. In any good group, someone can usually be found to fit each slot. See if you can recognize the following roles as having been played out in groups in which you participate.

- *The Mover*, the person who gets things done.
- *The Clown* keeps things from getting too heavy but also can inhibit seriousness when it is needed.
- *The Skeptic* raises tough questions just about the time the group is ready to get moving . . . or get carried away.
- *The Technician* has the answers, sometimes biblical, sometimes practical, sometimes technical. May not offer them unless asked and may not be very tactful.
- *The Encourager* builds others up and makes them feel valuable.
- *The Deviant* always seems to have to be different, but he or she may protect the group from the dangers of "group think"—even at the risk of expulsion.
- *The Nice Guy* does what is asked (especially the unsung jobs) without grumbling. But don't take this person for granted for too long.
- *The Leader* may be a role that is shared, rotated, or exercised in various styles, but beware of the claim that there is no leader. Behind-the-scenes leadership can be more manipulative than that which is out front and therefore accountable.

The Potential of "Fellowship Evangelism"

Recognizing the power of group fellowship to lovingly embrace people, some churches have organized small groups in hopes that they will be able to reach out evangelistically. Paul M. Miller has defined this as "fellowship evangelism."

> Fellowship evangelism refers to the deliberate effort by a fellowship group of a local church to surround unsaved persons with the warmth and power of Christian fellowship, and thereby lead them to a transforming encounter with the living Christ, and into membership in the church. It implies that each individual member will deliberately become a "friend of sinners," cultivating acquaintance and redemptive friendship with unsaved persons, then winning them into the circle of his or her own fellowship or study group in the church, and eventually to personal faith in Christ.[3]

He suggests further the evangelistic value of this type of outreach:

> Christians need to be informed that Christian fellowship does have evangelistic power. Many Christians do not realize this. They have been conditioned to think that preaching draws persons to Christ, that Christian service exemplifies Christ, that Christian worship has drawing power, and that verbal Christian testimony convinces people and points them to Christ. But many have never been told that the mere presence of Christ among his own has a magnetic pull upon an unsaved person coming into that group.
> Christians need to be emphatically reminded that Christ is present in the midst of his own people and an unsaved person cannot come into that group without confronting Christ, even though no "religious" conversation is carried on.[4]

Certainly the demonstration quality of small groups is a powerful testimony of the kingdom in action. It is important to be able to say, "Come and see," as Christians love one another through helping each other in such things as reroofing a house, providing meals after the birth of a new baby, caring for the children, sharing money, cars, bearing some spiritual burden, or trying to break free from the power of alcoholism.

It's even more important for that Christian group to reach out to share the same fellowship and love with the unbelievers.

The Limitations of the Small Group

But in the long run several churches have found that small group *meetings*, per se, are not as good a tool for direct evangelistic outreach as was once thought.

David A. Womack, the pastor of Twin Palms Assembly of God in San Jose, California, says that small groups "are for *in*reach, not outreach!" He claims that the role of small groups is most effective in prayer and encouragement to its *members* to reach out to their friends and relatives with Christ's love, but not necessarily by inviting them into the inner sanctum of the small group.[5]

One of the reasons that fellowship groups and covenant groups—the kinds of groups where *koinonia* is strongest and should be most dramatic—do not in themselves constitute good tools for evangelism, is that it is difficult for them to assimilate new people. It takes time to build trust and intimacy, and new people can threaten the group's integrity and cohesion. However, once the group is secure, visitors can be judiciously introduced occasionally and in small numbers.

Inclusive Groups

Prayer groups, on the other hand, can usually handle new people, but they normally attract other Christians—those who are unattached or unhappy with their present church. Prayer groups are unlikely to be the first thing a non-Christian attends.

The Bible study group and the house church may want to attract newcomers, and they will be ideal for reaching some, but they can also intimidate the uninitiated. Some new people want to be warmly greeted, but then they prefer the anonymity of numbers when it comes to trying to sing unfamiliar songs or find books in the Bible. They may even want to be able to slip out of a meeting unnoticed if things get "too heavy." This is why the celebration or the all-church worship service can be the most comfortable place to invite some people. However, as Becky Pippert points out:

> Sooner or later we must get our non-Christian friends reading the Bible. One effective way is to gather several skeptic friends with one or two Christians and study a passage that vitally confronts us with the person of Christ. . . .
>
> When you invite your friends, assure them that no previous Bible knowledge is necessary. They do not have to believe in God or the Bible. The point is for them to read firsthand what the Bible actually says.[6]

The Challenge of Growth

One other challenge any group must face when aspiring to reach new people is multiplication. How large can the group grow before it must become two groups? Many experts suggest that small groups work best when their size is between eight to twelve members.

Certainly when the group gets too big, the dynamics of intimacy—so important to good small-group functioning—cannot work. Take, for example, the limits of time. Suppose the group meets for a two-hour period once a week. If 30 minutes are spent in worship and a short devotional, another 20 for announcements and group planning, that leaves only 70 minutes for personal sharing, interaction, and prayer—less than six minutes per person.

At Reba Place Church in Evanston, Illinois, during the late '70s small groups ranged in size from 12 to 24 adult members, with the average around 16. It was just too many to allow the groups to be receptive to newcomers. People wanted to be open, but it got to the point where they unconsciously weren't very receptive. It seemed like each group was continually being asked if it could include just one more new person. When the size became unmanageable the group would divide like a cell—half staying, and half leaving to make up a new group.

But this method of multiplication was costly in terms of relationships with'in the group. No sooner would people get to know and trust one another deeply than they would be asked to say goodbye. In time, the emotional toll on the part of the members was a growing hesitation to invest so deeply in one another because they instinctively knew that their relationships would soon be ripped apart.

The following plan has proved more satisfactory:

> 1. *Group size is not to exceed twelve persons.* It is interesting to notice now how eagerly groups build their size to 12 because they know when that size is reached they are safe. The placement committee will not pester them to take anyone new. It has also removed some of the unconscious hesitation to reach out to new people. If they respond, there *will* be a place for them, but it won't disrupt your group.
>
> 2. *Groups are not expected to divide in order to expand.* Instead, one person or couple may be asked to leave a group to join with one or two from another group in forming the core of a new group. This means that the original groups can look forward to relative stability.
>
> 3. *New groups are formed from the annual discipleship class.* The new leaders drawn from various old groups head up new groups of new people in the context of the nine-month-long discipleship class. At the end of the class, those groups that are stable continue as permanent groups. The other new people move into open slots in old groups.

It is not a perfect plan, but it is proving to be a much more sensitive and effective way to assimilate substantial numbers of new people.

The Life-Cycle of a Small Group

Paul Smith from Broadway Baptist Church in Kansas City, Missouri, has identified four stages in the life cycle of a small group—*forming, storming, norming,* and *reforming.*[7] Like the life stages in our human development, an ounce of understanding can assuage a ton of anxiety.

Stage One: Forming

This period, which begins with the conception and birth of the group, typically includes a lot of excitement and usually a little fear. People are hopeful that all their needs will be met; they commonly think the other people in the group are the most wonderful people in the world. But they also wonder whether the group will be safe, whether it will ask too much of them, and whether they will be manipulated by the group.

It typically lasts one to two months.

Stage Two: Storming

This is the period of disillusionment and conflict. After the newness of the group wears off, members begin to assert themselves. Issues of power and trust arise.

One of the major lessons is that we can't *make* community happen any more than we can save ourselves. It is a gift of God, and only God—not community—can satisfy our needs.

Usually this period lasts several meetings.

Stage Three: Norming

This is the time of nurturing and investment in one another. It is the time when we get down to the business of fulfilling the vision of the small group.

It lasts one to three or more years.

Stage Four: Reforming

This is the experience of change, decline, and death. Smith says,

> We need not fear this if we believe in a theology of death and resurrection.
>
> More problems are caused by not understanding this stage than any other. We have difficulty accepting the fact that groups end, especially our group. While not all groups actually stop meeting after this stage,

all must change.... After the needed changes occur, the cycle of birth, development, functioning, and death can start all over again. All long-term groups repeat this cycle many times.

Often this stage lasts from three to 18 months.

Understanding these strengths and weaknesses and dynamics of small groups can help us as we seek ways to let the fellowship we prize among ourselves be shared with others around us.

Our Message Includes Fellowship

When we think of our witness to the world, we need to remember that fellowship is not just a method of evangelism. It is part of our message. Christians proclaiming the gospel are inviting others to become one with them in Christ. The invitation is dramatized by the group life of the church. In turn the group members are strengthened to share that life with the non-Christian. But most important, in the fellowship of Christians lies the power which convinces the world of the truth of Christ and his good news.

Of this John Howard Yoder has written:

> The fellowship of Christians is not only the result of the proclamation of the gospel. It is also part of the content of the Christian message. There is therefore a basic contradiction in the idea that the gospel could be faithfully proclaimed by one person. If the "missionary" is a lone person or couple or a small and scattered team of workers, the world around them never sees the practice of moral and material mutual aid. Yet this was one of the most appealing factors in the witness of the early church.[8]

We Were Won by Fellowship

Our own coming to Christ was most likely through the dynamics of Christian fellowship. Dr. Win Arn, of the Institute for American Church Growth, surveyed 4,000 new Christians to learn how they first came to church:

1-2 percent were visited by members.
2-3 percent came because of the church programs.
3-4 percent came because of a special need.
3-4 percent came through a Sunday school class.
6-8 percent just walked in without prior contact.
8-12 percent were attracted by the pastor.
70-80 percent were invited by friends and relatives.[9]

But even beyond this research of how people first came to church, warm Christian fellowship has a broader impact. Robert T. Handy has written:

> Some of us were fortunate enough to find this in our own families. Some of us were caught up in the life of a Christian congregation which made known to us, however brokenly, something of the love of Christ and the meaning of Christian faith. Today there are millions who have not shared such an experience as yet, and who will believe the gospel only when they find it thus enacted in a specific church in their neighborhood.
>
> The world has many fellowships, countless casual associations, and a variety of rallies of all kinds. But a fellowship in which the presence of Christ is really felt, and in which the members feel themselves to have a real bond of kinship is a center of health and wholeness of the highest importance. A fellowship in which members are related to God and through his power to one another—that satisfies a human hunger that runs deep—so deep that many dare not recognize that they have it lest they fall into despair.
>
> Is your church and mine such a church as this? Most of us would probably have to reply with both a "yes" and a "no." Yes, for by God's grace the Spirit is at work in our midst. No, because we have resisted and grieved the Spirit. Yes, because the presence of Christ has been felt in our churches. No, because we do not keep our eyes on him and our ears tuned to hear his voice.[10]

For Group Discussion

1. Identify three different small groups in your church and locate them as closely as possible on the "Types of Small Groups" chart. Then discuss how the characteristics match up.

2. From the list of "roles" often operative in small groups, see if you can identify which ones are present in your primary small group.

3. On a scale from 1 to 5, with 5 being high, how inclusive is your small group? What other small groups in your church are more inclusive?

4. Have you been in a small group that faced Stage 4 in the small group life cycle? What happened?

5. Considering the ways people commonly come to church for the first time, share how each person in your group came to the church.

CHAPTER TEN

Discipling
for Maturity

In Chapter 8 we spoke of the importance of basing our witness in a life of *discipleship*. This chapter addresses one particular aspect of discipleship—bringing new believers to a level of relative maturity.

Our growth in Christ never ends in this life. But there is a critical early period for new Christians when they need a particularly solid experience of Christian community.

No gardener assumes, after plowing, raking, planting, and watching the first green life appear, that there is nothing more to do. No parents consider, after a healthy child is born, that their responsibility ceases. How often, though, newborn souls are left to weather their temptations alone, to find as best they can the spiritual food they need.

All of us have seen this happen with a frequency that must rebuke us sharply. For instance, Roger accepted Christ at the church summer camp that the youth director had urged him to attend. As long as he was surrounded by the friendly atmosphere of camp, he had the group support he needed.

But when he came home, things were different. The kids who accepted him at camp were from different towns. But those who had come from his home town church had their own close gang of which Roger had never been a part. No one deliberately excluded Roger. But he had always hung around with a different circle in high school, and the Christian kids simply didn't think of making a real effort to include him. Roger was not the kind of person to force his way into a group.

But a guy has to have friends. His old gang were still glad to see him, though they rode him a little for having "gotten religion." At first, he honestly tried to maintain his Christian life. (He had been strongly counseled at camp of the dangers of slipping back into some of the destructive patterns of his old way of life.) But eventually he wasn't able to stand alone for what he knew was right. In spite of his sincere intentions, he returned to drinking, snorting a little coke, and hanging out so late that he didn't get any homework done—it was the same old thing. He became thoroughly disgusted with himself and was convinced that he lacked the ability to live the Christian life.

By that time the kids in the church decided that his camp profession was nothing more than a mountaintop experience— not a real commitment to Christ. Consequently, there was no reason to include him in their group even if the idea had crossed their mind.

The Open-Back-Door Syndrome . . . Again

But that's not only a problem for cliquish teens. Adults have their own ways of not really incorporating a new person. It may not appear so blatant, but in time the new person becomes weary and drifts off. It is another aspect of the open-back-door syndrome.

Phyllis and Dale are an example. They were won to Christ through the witness and work of a congregation in the Northwest. They were warmly welcomed to the Sunday school and made to feel at home in worship services. But nobody thought of inviting them over for dinner. No one dropped by during the week for an informal visit. They were excluded, through sheer thoughtlessness, from hunting trips, shared shopping trips, and gift exchanges. For them the fellowship of the church was what happened on Sunday mornings and evenings. When they left the church door, they left the fellowship.

It wasn't long—about two months—before they left for good. The church missed them with nothing more than the comment: "Even though they have left us, we should not cease to pray for them."

Doesn't God Keep?

"Why can't we simply trust God to help new people grow?" someone wants to know. God has promised to keep those who believe, it is true, and God does keep. However, God's power to mature new believers—like the power to save—uses men and women as human instruments to work the divine will. Our understanding of how God saves souls has progressed far beyond the days when a respected church leader told William Carey, "Sit down, young man! When it pleaseth the Lord to convert the heathen, he will do it without your help or mine." Is it any less a misunderstanding of our responsibility to entrust the maturing of a newborn soul entirely to God without seeking to know how God wants us to help?

What Every New Believer Needs

What was missing for Roger and the couple from the Northwest? They needed to be received into a group "cell" in the body of Christ and nurtured toward maturity. While some small groups are not ideal for certain kinds of evangelism, small-group life is prime soil for helping a new believer grow.

Kevin M. Thompson, in his manual for small-group ministry, points out that in the Bible we are instructed to . . .

- open our lives to one another
- share our needs with one another

- confess our faults to one another
- forgive one another
- build up one another
- reprove, exhort, and rebuke one another
- bear one another's burdens
- be devoted to one another
- submit to one another
- minister gifts to one another
- love one another fervently
- have fellowship with one another
- serve one another.[1]

How can we do any of those things without significant, deep, and long-term relationships with one another? Bringing new people into small groups can facilitate these kind of relationships. Small groups provide a supportive community of friends who know us as we really are. Committed, trusting relationships develop as we share our lives and minister to one another's needs. In a small group people find a few others they can identify with, understand, and relate to consistently.

Those who are won to Christ should not have to face the problems of living the new life alone. A child learns habits, appreciations, and attitudes by living within a family—rather than in a formal teaching situation. Similarly, a new Christian learns the truths of Christian life and grows in them best by living together with other Christians in the family of God.

Growth toward Christian maturity is not an individual affair. It is a process of being joined together with others in the body of Christ so that, as Paul says, we can be "built up until we all reach unity in the faith and in the knowledge of the Son of God and become mature, attaining to the whole measure of the fullness of Christ" (Eph. 4:12-13). To attain that goal, we work together, new believers and more experienced Christians mutually enriching one another.

The kind of spiritual growth that is needed is three dimensional: toward God, toward one another, and toward the world.

1. Growth Toward God...

We think first, and rightly so, of helping new believers grow toward God. For this, group fellowship is essential.

In Gratitude

Together as we come to God, we continue to ask and to receive forgiveness for our individual and our group sins. And in so doing we feel increased appreciation for God's redeeming love in Christ. Such gratitude nurtures Christian life and faith.

The God who prefaced commandments to Israel with the reminder, "I am the Lord your God, who brought you out of Egypt, out of the land of slavery," bases his plea for the full loyalty of every Christian on the remembrance of his mercies. The New Testament practice of frequently breaking bread together continually reminded the redeemed of the cost of their redemption and of the love which provided the sacrifice. Our reminding one another over and over again of God's mercies will lead to an attitude of appreciation that wants to give in return a life of service and faithfulness.

Remembering God's mercies deepens our trust in God for the present and the future. When together we seek renewed forgiveness, speak or sing or pray our thanksgiving for salvation, and show our appreciation by sharing the bread and wine of communion, we help one another to declare confidently, "He who did not spare his own Son, but gave him up for us all—how will he not also, along with him, graciously give us all things?" (Rom. 8:32).

In Communion

Group fellowship can lead individuals into closer personal communion with God. Newborn souls may need help in learning to live in the presence of God, in studying the Bible, and in developing a meaningful prayer life.

Also, young Christians can often inspire older ones by their enthusiasm for God's Word and their joy in prayer.

Guidance in Bible study, prayer, and fellowship with God may be given through formal instruction. But the sharing of experiences informally in the context of small groups is frequently more effective.

A group of students in a Christian high school asked a teacher to lead them in a weekly prayer fellowship. The meeting was informal and extremely simple. Week after week, all of the students exchanged testimonies. They shared with each other Scriptures through which the Holy Spirit had spoken to them in their private devotional meditations during the week. Then they prayed together about individual problems and mutual concerns.

Sometimes the teacher wondered whether the meeting had much significance for the students and felt that a systematic plan of Bible study might have been more meaningful. But some years later, several who had shared in this fellowship agreed without hesitation that the one factor which contributed most to their spiritual growth in high school was the mutual exchange in this small fellowship.

"Many times," one said, "I would have grown careless about my personal Bible study and prayer if I had not known I would be expected to share with the others something I had gained. Hearing what the others had to say was often very helpful. But the greatest value I received was help in disciplining myself to have regular and meaningful personal devotions."

In Christian Discipline

Together, too, we grow in Christian discipline and in our understanding of its meaning in terms of everyday life. Young Christians may in all sincerity surrender themselves completely to God without having a clear understanding of what this means in terms of daily activities and attitudes. "I thought I was wholly consecrated to God, but now the Holy Spirit is showing me that ..." is a testimony that has been repeated many times by growing Christians.

The fact that one has received new light on what is involved in following Christ need not discredit the reality of one's former dedication to God. In a sense it is true that consecration is a once-for-all experience of surrender to God for all of life, with no secret reservations to turn back if the cost becomes too great. On the other hand, no follower of Christ can possibly foresee all the demands that God's way will place on one's life. Therefore, consecration is also a day-by-day decision to do God's will as it is revealed in each situation.

This ever-growing concept of the claim of Christ upon every area of the Christian's life is best learned and tested in the context of fellowship with other Christians who acknowledge that claim and act upon it continually. The good missionary Barnabas took his first recorded step toward total consecration when he was part of the fellowship of Spirit-filled believers who counted nothing they possessed as their own.

2. Growth Toward One Another ...

When we are helping one another grow toward God, we grow in our relationship with each other. Likewise fellowship with other Christians deepens our fellowship with God, and communion with God enriches our communion with other Christians.

The New Testament pictures of the church emphasize the mutual interaction of growth in these two directions. The church is a holy temple of God in which each believer is a *living stone*. It is a *body* of which Christ is the head and every believer a member. It is the *flock* of God with Christ as Chief Shepherd. It is the *family* of our Father God, and Christ is our elder brother. The *bride* of Christ, the *household* of God, *branches* of God's vine, *salt* of the earth, and *light* of the world—with such varied metaphors the New Testament describes the life and work of Christ.

In Loyalty

It is easy to build an emotional kind of loyalty to the beautiful ideal of the invisible church as pictured in the figurative language of the New Testament. The invisible church is the church universal, all believers everywhere, not one confined by walls, membership, or even geography. True loyalty, however, includes loyalty to specific people, to the local congregation, the visible church, with all its imperfections. Those who mature in Christ through the fellowship of small church groups have received good preparation for loyalty to the congregation.

In Understanding

In the church we learn quickly that Christians, though redeemed, often need to come to God and to one another for forgiveness. Therefore, it does not need to be a bitter disappointment to discover that a congregation can and does make mistakes and that it sometimes fails to reflect Christ perfectly.

We will be spared the shock of the teenager who had accepted Christ at a mission church quite far from the parent congregation. Her first year as a boarding student in a church school, where for the first time she lived among Christians her own age, was a decided letdown. "I thought all Christians were like Margaret and Ruth," she said, naming the mature Christian women who worked in the mission where she had found Christ. But of course many were not so mature, and it was hard for her to get over that disillusionment.

In Unity

Life together in a loving Christian fellowship also prepares new Christians to expect and to value differing opinions among believers. In the small group they can hear Christians exchange ideas, disagree in friendly fashion, and learn from one another. In the group fellowship they can learn by example that the best way to study the Bible is with open minds and readiness to be taught by the Spirit through one another. They feel the true spiritual unity of those determined to know and obey the will of God even though they may not have identical interpretations of what is required.

With this experience of unity in the small group, new believers will not expect that unity is synonymous with uniformity. The New Testament recognizes diversities of gifts, administration, and operation under the control of one Lord, one body, and one Spirit.

In Responsibility

As new Christians grow in relationship to other believers and in loyalty to the church, we need to help them hear the call to do their share of the work of the church. Unless we help them to learn, few new converts will understand that every believer has been called to a place of responsibility which only they can fill.

In the family of God, as in any well-ordered household, duties are shared according to the strength and ability of each member. Gradually new members can be led to accept responsibility in the church. Wise leaders, in addition to providing formal training in leadership, will watch for opportunities to put new members to work.

This should not be done in a haphazard fashion—expecting every able body to teach Sunday school or scolding the congregation in general for not joining the evangelism team. Help-

ing people discover their spiritual gifts is the basis upon which
recruitment for ministries and the assignment of tasks should
be made in the church.

While searching for ways to help people discover and use
their spiritual gifts, C. Peter Wagner read 48 books on the subject, and yet he believed there was room for one more. There
remains a tragic ignorance among many believers concerning
where they fit into the body of Christ, and how they can
contribute. In his book, *Your Spiritual Gifts Can Help Your
Church Grow*, Wagner says, "Not everybody has spiritual gifts
[as he has defined them]. Unbelievers do not. But every Christian person who is committed to Jesus and truly a member of
his body has at least one gift, or possibly more."[2]

Because they do not understand this, many Christians
remain idle. Our task is to help new believers realize that the
church exists, not to comfort and cuddle them, but to do God's
work in the world, and that, as members of the church, each
one has a way to contribute.

A study of spiritual gifts and a systematic identification of
these gifts in the context of small groups where each person is
known is one of the best ways to help people take their *appro-
priate* responsibility in the church.

3. Growth Toward The World . . .

This is the third dimension of growth in Christian maturity—growth toward the world. Christians who draw close to
Christ hear his, "Go into all the world." As they develop true
loyalty to his church, they accept their share of its mission. This
includes wholehearted support of the organized mission program of the church as well as a concern to witness personally in
everyday contacts.

Alert leaders can do much to encourage convictions for missionary work and personal witness. Mission sermons, special mission-week emphases, mission studies, mission-centered Sunday and Bible school lessons—all are important. But even more essential is the contagious missionary enthusiasm of a committed group of Christians, who care enough to surrender time, money, talents, and self for the service of Christ. Without this, the best teaching will avail nothing.

A pastor who has opposed his daughter's going to school to prepare for a church assignment abroad need not preach any sermons on the great commission. The book of Acts cannot be taught by Sunday school teachers who, for love of comfort and security, stifle their own convictions to move as self-supporting workers to a remote congregational outpost by arguing that a person can serve the Lord at home.

The Best Safeguard

If we can help each new believer to grow in relationship with God, in fellowship with the church, and in responsibility to the world, we will not need to erect artificial barriers to separate the church from the world.

Indeed, unless this growth is continually taking place, the most carefully constructed wall will be neither strong enough or high enough to keep the world's evil from infiltrating the church. In physical life the best protection against disease is the resistance of a strong healthy body. In the church the best safeguard against worldliness is the church's own vigorous life, which is continually inbreathed by the Holy Spirit.

It is extremely difficult, perhaps impossible, for people to commit themselves to Jesus and grow in him without being a part of a local body of believers. One cannot be joined to the head (Christ) without being joined to his body. The life of the head is supplied and transferred through the body to its various members. Through small groups people find a doorway into the life of the Christian fellowship and remain in Christ, joined to his body in committed small-group relationships.

For Group Discussion

1. Share an incident you know of (without revealing the identification of the person) where someone became a Christian but was not "socialized" into the church and thereby fell away.

2. Discuss what you think about how God keeps. Does God need (use) us to keep people? What happens when we are not available? Explain and relate your answer to Ephesians 4:13.

3. Why is gratitude an important spiritual virtue? What happens when it is absent?

4. What do you think of loyalty? Does a person need to be a part of a tangible body of believers? What happens if the person is not? How far should loyalty go?

Witness: Mission

In mission the church answers the call to unite with God's loving, creative, liberating purposes in the world. The church receives gifts of the Spirit, discerning both personal and congregational direction, and commits itself in loving obedience to ministries of evangelism, service, peace, and justice.

CHAPTER ELEVEN

Family-to-Family Evangelism

James Dobson of Focus on the Family is concerned to reach, teach, and support families. When asked, "What frustrates you most about family ministry?" he said, "I wish I could convince my fellow Christians that the most productive form of outreach is right under our noses! Passing out tracts and knocking on doors have their place.... But nothing links families to Christ like linking them to the established community of faith.... Even though we attend a friendly church, I occasionally become irritated by the lack of dedicated workers in this critical task of *caring* for people. It is, in my opinion, the most important family ministry a church can implement."[1]

Tom Eisenman, author of *Everyday Evangelism*, claims that our mission begins with who we are, where we are, and who we're with. "The church is the people of God. Everywhere God's people go, the church goes. The church's mission is to represent the kingdom of God in the world. Paul proclaims the great mandate for the church when he writes, "God was reconciling the world to himself in Christ, not counting men's sins against them. And he has committed to us the message of reconciliation. We are therefore Christ's ambassadors, as though God were making his appeal through us' (2 Cor.5:19-20)."[2]

Salvation Appeal

The apostle Paul describes the effect we as believers should have as we go about our daily lives in our neighborhoods, with our families, at work: "But thanks be to God, who ... through us spreads everywhere the fragrance of the knowledge of him. For we are to God the aroma of Christ among those who are being saved" (2 Cor. 2:14-15).

Paul calls this the aroma of Christ. Eisenman calls this salvation appeal. He tells this story:

> A young woman came to talk•with me one day about joining the leadership development class I was starting in our congregation.
>
> When I asked her how she became a Christian, she told me an interesting story. She said that she came to the University of Colorado out of high school, and when she arrived in Boulder she needed to find part-time work. Her first job was waiting tables at the Boulder Country Club.
>
> Out of all the people she waited on regularly, there was one couple who consistently treated her differently. They always engaged her in conversation, asking her questions about herself and her family. They were concerned about how she was getting along during her first year away from home. They communicated real interest in her.
>
> After finding out that they were members of our congregation, she dropped in to worship one Sunday morning. It was just what she needed. The Lord did his work. In a few weeks she was in a new member's class, and soon she decided to follow Christ.
>
> The couple she told me about have what I like to call salvation appeal. There is something about who they are and what they do that draws unbelievers to Christ.[3]

The Witness of a Christian Family

The most close-knit subgroup of the church to which any Christian can belong is the family. In such intimate fellowship exists a powerful, but frequently overlooked, means of evangelism.

Starting at home seemed to be a crucial component of the witness of the early apostles. Robert Coleman, in *The Master Plan of Discipleship*, says, "Special attention was given to reaching the head of the house, who when convinced of the claims of Christ, became the means of winning the family, as

with the Philippian jailer (Acts 16:25-34). In the case of Corne-
lius, his household included not only relatives but friends and
servants (Acts 10:7, 22-48). With Lydia, probably an unmarried
woman supporting a household, the slaves or freedmen in the
house followed her example in the faith (Acts 16:14-15)."[4]

It's important to remember that with our family, just as with
anyone, we must bring the Christian message in a loving, caring, and sensitive way, rather than being judgmental and con-
demning. Tom Eisenman says this was a lesson he learned the
hard way:

> Judie and I were students at the University of Wisconsin when we
> became Christians in October during my senior year. We were excited
> about our new faith in Christ, and we had been witnessing to my
> parents who lived near us. It was about two weeks before Christmas
> when we heard a knock on the back door of the little house we were
> renting. I opened the door. My dad was there, banging the snow off
> his boots. He came in, sat at our table, and told us he had a very hard
> thing to say. He couldn't even look us in the eyes as he spoke. "We
> don't want you to come home this Christmas. If you're there, you'll
> just spoil things for the rest of us."
>
> His words came as a complete shock. My dad is one of the most lov-
> ing, gentle men I've ever known, and our family has always been
> close. Something dreadful had to be happening for him to face us with
> the news that we were not welcome at the most precious family cele-
> bration we shared. What was it?
>
> In just two brief months between my conversion and my dad's visit,
> I had managed to totally alienate my entire family. My dad's words
> pointed out in no uncertain terms how I had failed to demonstrate to
> my family the newfound love I claimed.
>
> For openers, I remember thinking that what they needed most was
> to know that they were going to hell. I told them this right away, for
> their own good. After that I made it clear that I could no longer hang
> around with them because their bad influence might rub off on me.
> And when it got closer to Christmas, I just had to let them know that
> the way they celebrated Christ's birthday, with drinking and gluttony,
> was sinful.
>
> I can almost laugh about this today. Think of it. Everything was al-
> ways fine in our family before. Then suddenly, there I was, the son my

parents had poured twenty years of effort and sacrifice into, telling them that their lives really amounted to nothing and that all the family activities I had enjoyed throughout my life now showed up on my long list of mortal sins.

Fortunately Christ's love broke through. Judie and I asked if we could come over and meet with everybody a few days before Christmas. I did the first loving thing in my family since becoming a Christian. I asked my whole family to forgive me for being so incredibly arrogant and judgmental. We shared tears together. It was the beginning of a new relationship. . . .[5]

The Witness of Hospitality

The witness of a Christian family to others often begins with the way we share our home. Read through the names in your guest book. Or list the persons you have invited during the last year for dinner or for a friendly evening. Unless you have made a special effort to be inclusive, the chances are that the same names keep recurring like a soothing refrain. Unless you are an unusual host or hostess, most of the guests you keep inviting, perhaps all of them, are Christians.

One of the requirements for a church leader is hospitality (1 Tim. 3:2; Tit. 1:8). Joe Aldrich, author of *Lifestyle Evangelism*, says, "Note especially the word 'hospitable.' The Greek term literally means 'a lover of strangers.' Now, we often invite fellow Christians over to eat or talk, but are they the strangers of this passage? Is it not more realistic to understand the term as characterizing church leaders who invite their non-Christian neighbors over so they can get acquainted?"[6]

Of course we want to open our homes to our friends and family. But why not build friendships with those who do not know Christ? Invite a neighbor, a co-worker from the office, the parents of your child's best friend at school. It need not be an elaborate guest meal. Just an evening of fellowship may begin a friendship which will lead to an effective witness for Christ. If you feel you don't have much in common, or conversation might be awkward, playing a popular board game, followed with dessert, may break the ice. A Christian experienced in witness through friendship wrote, "Often, after a well-planned evening has been enjoyed, with creative and stimulating activity, non-Christians have commented that it has been the best evening they've had in years, and they were glad to realize that people could have a good time without drinking."[7]

Lois and Bob Shuford have a caroling party every Christmas. They invite several members and their families from church—plus an equal number of neighbor families. The mix of people is stimulating over hot cider and cookies after caroling. This is a good chance for church members to share fellowship with others, and neighbors to meet the Shufords' church family.

At Reba Place Church in Evanston, Illinois, some members double the amount of food their family needs for Sunday dinner. Then they look for opportunities to invite visitors to come home with them for a meal after the worship service. Nothing insures a repeat visit like being included in a family dinner on one's first visit to a church!

Families who live near a university have a unique opportunity to reach out to international students. These bright young people are eager for friendship and the opportunity to know Americans personally. Many are far away from home and welcome a chance to spend holidays with a local family.

One host evaluated their experience:

> Besides learning to know about the countries and the religion of these our friends, we ate some of their food: Filipino dishes, Indian curry, and others. They in turn were glad to share our hospitality and our food, and though we didn't insist, they did come to our church as well. We in turn learned more about being friends for Christ than in many courses on evangelism. We found that we could share Christ in a very simple, unaffected, and natural way. We learned that these students, representing many thousands who are presently in America,

appreciate the kind of friendship that our families offered. We in turn appreciated their friendship. We want to repeat the experience."[8]

Showing Christ's Love to Children

When sharing Christ's love through hospitality, don't forget your children's friends. Karen Burton Mains shares this story in her book, *Open Heart, Open Home*:

> Coming downstairs one day, arms loaded with soiled sheets and blankets, I nudged my way around two little forms huddled in conference on the treads. *Why do children love stairs so much?*
>
> Excusing myself, we shifted positions a bit, and I balanced my load on its way to the washer in the basement. I had not gone too far when I heard a little voice pipe, "I love to come to your house. Your mother doesn't yell all the time the way my mother does."
>
> It gave me pause, and I suddenly realized this little girl had been around frequently. I didn't know her mother so I hadn't any way to judge the comment about yelling, but I did sense she had found shelter, a quiet space in a noisy world. *You are welcome, child, to my stairway any time.*

Recently Jack and Nellie's college-age son, home for the Christmas holidays, asked if his friend Cal could come over for dinner. "He just got kicked out of his house," Jim said briefly. Over the next few days, Cal made a few attempts to patch things up with his mom, but the situation didn't budge. Dinner turned into a ten-day visit, including Christmas day.

Twelve-year-old Ruth wasn't sure she liked that. "Christmas is supposed to be for family! We don't have any presents for him! Grandma and Grandpa will be here!"

"I know," sympathized Nellie. "But we don't want there to be 'no room in our inn' at Christmas time."

Cal, who considers himself an agnostic, shared in the Advent celebration each night around the table, and went to church with the family. Who can tell what seeds were sown? But hospitality for his friend was not lost on Jim. "Thanks, Mom and Dad, for welcoming Cal so freely. It means a lot to me."

There are many lonely, hurting children around us—from families broken by divorce. Some Christian families living in the country open their homes for several weeks each summer to children from the inner city. Lasting and redemptive friendships have grown from such small beginnings. Christian couples who have a heart for children and room may want to consider being foster parents, or even adopt an older child who is considered "unadoptable." These are not small decisions. All of us must consider how we can obey Jesus' teaching to "Let the little children come to me, and do not hinder them, for the kingdom of God belongs to such as these" (Mark 10:14).

Children are fertile ground for the seeds of God's love. One young adult recently affirmed the seeds planted in his own life by Christian families: "My father left us before I was two. By the time I was a teenager, I had done a lot of things I'm not proud of. Nevertheless, two of my high school friends reached out to me. As they shared their families with me, I decided that I wanted to share their faith. What can the church do to help single parents? Reach out to their children. Let them see strong families. Give them hope."[8]

Another young woman agrees. "My father was killed in the war when I was five, and my mother raised us three children alone. With all my heart I believe that the greatest contribution the church could make to single parents would be for a person of the sex of the missing parent to 'adopt' the children for periods of time (a weekend once a month, perhaps, or an evening). The church failed my brother in this—and never let it be forgotten that little girls need fathers, too."[10]

Reach Out to Single Parents

There are many single parents today, but most of them find it difficult to know where they fit in, even—or especially—in the church. They feel awkward in couples' groups. Yet, as the parents of children, they don't quite fit with the singles either. Too often they feel isolated.

For hurting men and women who have experienced the trauma and rejection of a failed relationship, the last thing they need is rejection from the church. "When my son was severely injured two years ago," one mother shared, "I was over-whelmed by the outpouring of support. A pastor visited almost every day. People sent flowers and cards. Many brought casseroles. And hundreds of people prayed! Samuel was mentioned in the Sunday pastoral prayer for weeks, and this in a church with 2,000 members. In contrast, when our husband and father walked out on us more than a year ago, there were no calls or visits from pastors or others, and no real prayer support. There was one notable exception. A friend from church came over and sat with me for a while right after my husband moved his things out of the house. Her visit was a tremendous encouragement."[11]

How can we reach out to single parents? One parent suggested: "Don't say, 'We'll have to get together.' Rather, 'Are you free to stop over tonight?' Set up a time. I'd like to get out of the house. Don't just talk to me on Sunday. Call me during the week to say, 'Hi. Do you need help?' Don't say, 'I don't know how you do it. The Lord is gracious.' Rather, 'I'm free Saturday morning or Tuesday night. You can drop the kids off for a while.' Time alone is precious."[12]

Advantages of Family Friendships

Family-to-family friendship, whether single-parent or two-parent families, has a twofold advantage. It is true that a child playing alone with children of parents who do not know Christ may be influenced by wrong values. Even a Christian teenager may lack courage to stand for what is right among friends who laugh at his or her beliefs. This danger is minimized (though certainly not eliminated) when the friendships are built on a family-to-family sharing of activities. When time is given to communication and friendship with the parents of our children's friends, the non-Christian parents often come to respect and appreciate the values of Christian parents.

Furthermore, those won to Christ by this method will have family support as they begin to live for God. All of us have witnessed the struggles of young Christians whose families have not yet found Christ, even when parents are not hostile to Christianity. We are well aware, too, of the tragedy of the many promising Sunday school and summer Bible school pupils who lose interest as they grow older. If Christian families can win other families to Christ, then children and young people will have the advantages of Christian home life.

Follow the Moving Van

Newcomers moving into our communities bring special opportunity for witness. When you make the first friendly call on the new neighbors down the street, your offer of friendship may include an invitation to church and Sunday school. If they have attended church, you can direct them or offer to take them to the nearest church of their denomination. If they do not attend church, you may help get them started by assuring them that they would be welcome in yours.

Dramatize Your Love in Actions

Thoughtful persons can find many ways of showing Christ's love to their neighbors—a pot of soup for a family who's got the flu, an evening of baby-sitting for parents who rarely have a chance to go away together, help with putting on a new roof. But we can't do this if all we do is wave in passing, and don't know their needs. We have to take time to chat over the back fence, or knock on the other apartment doors in our building, and borrow (or lend) that common cup of sugar.

> A man dropped in to see an old German neighbor across the street one day and the elderly man proudly showed his [garden] truck patch, flourishing in the midst of drought. He explained that he watered his half acre of vegetables mostly by hand, although he was eighty-two years old. "What a job!" the friend exclaimed. "It's too much work for a man of your years. You and your wife don't need all those vegetables."
>
> "No," he said, "ve do it vor de neighbors. Ve grow goot friends in de garten, ja?" and he laughed as he loaded his neighbor's arms with cucumbers and tomatoes.
>
> Using similar terminology we can bake good friends, crochet good friends, and . . . while our hands are busy, we can spend our moments in thought and prayer to God and for those we endeavor to reach. [13]

In every community there are persons to whom Christian families can minister. Too often feelings of goodwill are crowded into the holiday season. At Thanksgiving or Christmas we collect food for the needy, bring flowers to the old and ill, wrap gifts for orphans, and sing for those in institutions. Though these efforts are good, they would be more effective spread out. A shut-in would enjoy regular visits more than a surplus of food or flowers one week a year. A special Christmas treat and a program do not mean as much to lonely persons as having year-round friends who will sometimes take them for a drive, invite him to dinner, or offer to run small errands. The children of the poor family down the street do not need a load of Christmas toys so much as they need kindness and attention 52 weeks of the year.

Be Ready to Receive

As we show kindness to neighbors, we should keep in mind that constantly receiving help can be painful for sensitive persons. It is unpleasant to feel continually in debt to another.

All of us know the embarrassment of having a friend force some favor or gift upon us and refuse to accept anything in return. In the same way our best-intentioned kindnesses may complicate our relationships to those we wish to help. Playing Lord and Lady Bountifuls in the neighborhood, we may unconsciously build barriers to real friendships. For friendship to be true and mutual there must be a sharing—a willingness both to receive and to give.

It may be as simple as accepting neighbors' help just as naturally as you would make the offers to them, or asking advice in an area where they have expert knowledge. Your neighbors will be far more ready to accept the contributions you want to make to their life and experience if they know that sometimes they have opportunities to contribute to you. Many Christians have learned, quite by accident, that accepting help breaks down barriers.

Take Part in Community Projects

Neighborhood friendships can be built, too, as we share in wholesome school and community activities. Too often Christian families are so busy with church activities that we ignore activities and projects that affect our neighbors. Or we only make our voices known when we are unhappy about something. Our disapproval would be a more effective witness if we were also known for enthusiastic support of all projects in which we can conscientiously participate. Christian and non-Christian parents can find common interest in parent-teachers' associations, children's playground projects, and the like. All good citizens, whether Christian or not, should be interested in community cleanup campaigns, aid to the underprivileged, war upon disease, and the battle against prejudice. Working together at such activities, we will learn to know one another better.

Dig Deeper Than the Surface

There are no shortcuts to friendship. To reach out to our neighbors—and allow them to reach out to us—demands effort and self-denial. We have to consciously dig deeper than the surface. Even those with whom we converse freely about externals do we rarely know well enough to discuss ideas and values. Our conversation does not get beneath the surface because we meet as acquaintances, not as friends, although we may have been neighbors for many years. Before we can talk intimately, as friend to friend, we need to build friendship. Until this happens, our efforts to speak for Christ will seem forced and artificial, sandwiched between comments on the weather or why the mailman is so late today.

Hospitality—inviting our neighbors into our homes—is one way to begin to build closer friendships in which it becomes natural to share our deeper thoughts and feelings.

Be Ready to Share Christ

All of these ways of building meaningful and close relationships with neighbors can lead to opportunities to share Christ naturally as we exchange ideas about our work, interests, and aims. Telling what the Bible says about some problems we are working at together will open the way for further questions. This may lead to an invitation to meet with a few others for Bible study and discussion.

Many non-Christians are too frightened to accept an invitation to formal Bible study in a church building. To invite them for dinner and then suggest Bible study or prayer may make them feel resentful that they have been tricked into more than they bargained for. But if they have learned to love and trust us and if they see that the Bible has meaning and help for us, they may be ready to explore the possibility that their lives, too, can be enriched by its message.

Neighborhood Bible Study Groups

If opportunity for Bible study develops, the group should be kept small and unprofessional. For most of our neighbors such activity is a venture into the unknown. The leadership of a minister or a trained Bible teacher may frighten them into silence or to flight. They will feel more free in a situation where lay persons read the Bible together as equals and share ideas on what it says. The use of several modern translations, with a standard commentary for reference on any difficult passages, will enable any sincere group, however untrained, to have an interesting and profitable study under the Holy Spirit's guidance.

Let Your Light Shine

It is important that each Christian family live as Christians among their neighbors. Wherever Christian families live, family-to-family friendship can be a means of winning others to Christ. In your community you may discover such friendships to be the untried technique which will reach the lost who have resisted revival meetings, personal evangelism, and invitations to Sunday school. As was mentioned in a previous chapter, when Dr. Win Arn, of the Institute for American Church Growth, interviewed 4,000 new Christians to learn how they first came to church, 70 to 80 percent were invited by friends and relatives.

To let our light shine means that we live in such close contact with Christ, the greater light, that his glory is reflected in what we say and do. It means, too, that we live so close to those who do not know Christ that his light can penetrate their darkness.

For Group Discussion

1. Recall and share an incident when you may have related to a non-Christian in an unaccepting and arrogant manner.

2. Make a list of the persons you have invited during the last year for dinner or for a friendly evening. How many of them were non-Christians?

3. What qualities make your family "rich?" We often speak of the stewardship of our money and possessions, knowing God wants us to be generous, but what about the gifts that make our families rich? List one new way you could share a rich quality of your family with someone else. Set a date to do so.

4. List and discuss four things you need and can receive from your neighbors.

CHAPTER TWELVE

Welcoming the Weak and Needy[1]

We want to welcome all who come to our doors into the fellowship of Christ. But what does it really mean to welcome "all" into the assembly of believers?

Sarah Phillips was 27 and dying. She had ALS, a degenerative nerve disease that would soon kill her. The rehabilitation institute had done everything it could to help her cope with what was happening so rapidly in her body. But Sarah didn't want to spend her last weeks in an institution. She wanted to go home to her apartment for a couple weeks while her mother got ready to receive her, then spend her last days with her mother in another state. Arrangements were made for a nurse to be with her during the days, but Sarah was terrified of sleeping. Her father had died of ALS in his sleep less than a year earlier.

Sarah was not a Christian. But she had heard about Reba Place Church in Evanston, Illinois, from Jerry Bogatz a year earlier—before her disease was evident. Jerry, a member of Reba, stayed in contact with Sarah as the disease was diagnosed and began to progress. When the Bogatzes brought her to church, many people reached out to welcome her. One was Martha Cooper, a paraplegic who knew the agony of living in a body that did not function properly. When Sarah left the rehabilitation institute, she asked the Bogatzes if some women from the church could stay with her at night.

What about Sarah's request? The church could have helped pay for a room in a nursing home or encouraged her to move in with her mother sooner. Both options might have met their Christian duty, and they would have avoided disrupting anyone's schedule. But she had asked the church for personal care.

Would Sarah receive the Lord if the church cared for her? Who could know? It wasn't fair to respond on the basis of that expectation. There was only one legitimate question. Sarah had asked for the church's help; could the members give it?

After soberly considering the consequences, 16 women volunteered to spend the night with Sarah in teams of two. In some cases the volunteers had to find care for their own children. They adjusted their schedules, dropped out of other church obligations, and agreed to live with exhaustion the day after their turn. In addition, 17 other people joined a support team to pray for Sarah and the caregivers. Little by little a way was found, and a will to help emerged.

The volunteers usually stayed awake while Sarah slept. They calmed her panic when she awoke, communicated God's love to her, helped her talk about her impending death. They did every physical thing for her from feeding her to moving her foot to a more comfortable position. She was still able to talk and move her head. But there was always the possibility that Sarah's diaphragm would recieve no more signals to draw another breath.

The Long and Short of Ministry to the Needy

The task of ministering to Sarah seemed huge, but it also promised to be brief. Most of us can mobilize for short-term compassion. Ambivalence creeps in when it looks like we will be saddled with ongoing service to weak or disturbed people. How can we build a congregation of strong, mature saints if all the time and energy is devoured by needy people?

There is no lack of scriptural injunctions to receive and serve the poor, weak, and needy. Jesus "came to seek and to save what was lost" (Luke 19:10), "to preach good news to the poor," (Luke 4:18ff.), and our very salvation is tied to how we serve the least of Jesus' brothers (Matt. 25:34-46). But we usually expect those needy people to be quickly transformed into the strong and mature. What happens when they are not? What should we do when we foresee that the needy are likely to remain needy for a long time? How do we engineer a "balanced" congregation?

Like a growing number of churches today, Reba Place is divided into small groups of about a dozen people each. Every group has a designated leader plus several mature support people to help add stability. Then, into that context it is possible to invite new Christians, "weaker brothers and sisters," and needy, even disturbed, people.

It's been a good model, but the categories haven't always worked. The lines of distinction are not so neat. The strongest and most successful among the group are at times very needy. And those viewed as basically needy have come through with gifts just when they were needed most.

Martha, for instance, was one of the primary organizers for the ministry to Sarah, even though Martha is confined to a wheelchair. Her handicap has developed in her a strength of character and compassion unequaled in many people. Michele, a nurse, was another organizer. And yet she was a single parent who had received much support from others in the church.

In more recent times the church has been paying less attention to who is or isn't "needy" and more attention to spiritual gifts. The biblical analogy of the church as a body indicates that each member has a vital role, each member needs *all* the other members, and those members who appear less comely are actually to be most highly esteemed.

Recognition of spiritual gifts still enables the church to be careful when organizing small groups, but it does not see ministry as a one-way street.

Intolerance of the Weak and Needy

In spite of agreement among many Christians concerning what we *ought* to do, it is sometimes hard to welcome the weak. We fear that if we really open up our arms, we will become a magnet for overwhelming numbers of needy people. Love is so rare in this world that there is some cause for that concern. At Reba they have *not* been able to incorporate all the people who have come to them. At times they have felt overwhelmed and have had to put on the brakes. They just can't put everyone into small groups, the basic ministry setting.

But there are other, more insidious reasons for repelling the weak and needy.

1. We don't want to turn off the successful and the gifted. Modern marketing philosophy tells us a congregation filled with educated professionals will probably attract similar people. After all, who wants to associate with losers?

When one looks around Reba's congregation on Sunday morning, there are usually a dozen or more from the Ridgeview, a local sheltered-care home for the mentally retarded. Several are in wheelchairs. There are Central American refugees, a large group of Cambodian refugees, whites, a few blacks, and orientals—a real mix.

One member admitted: "I squirmed the day a man rolled in in his wheelchair wearing a big floppy hat with campaign and PTL buttons all around it. Lavender and chartreuse feathers hung down in his eyes, and a dirty serape was thrown over his shoulders. He smelled from ten feet away, and on the back of his chair was a bag with what looked like a bone in it. A sign on the bag read, 'In case of seizure.'

"I couldn't prevent the worry that something embarrassing was going to happen, and I wondered how often our ragtag assembly offended the more refined visitors."

2. *We want a powerful, transforming religion.* Spiritual success can become an even more coveted goal than physical success for some church people. Is our faith powerful if so many of our people are emotionally disturbed, retarded, crippled, and even sinful? It's easy to feel that way. We can wonder, "Does our God reign?"

One Sunday after a teaching on prayer, one member at Reba got up and suggested that the congregation pray seriously for Sarah's physical healing. Sarah was not present, but did they dare take such a public risk? What if God did not heal her? What if she died? Where was the spiritual power?

The congregation *did* pray, a simple, direct request to God. They asked that God heal and save her life. They made no claims of knowing God's will and did not demand that he grant their request, but they let God know what they fervently wished.

3. *We don't like to count ourselves among the truly needy.* Could it be that God leaves some obviously handicapped people in our midst, unhealed, to remind us that we are all needy, but able to give? That has been one impact on congregations that have welcomed the handicapped. If that is the case, we owe the handicapped people a great debt. Because without a consciousness of our own weakness, we could lose our sense of dependence on God. And that would be disastrous.

But it is human nature to want to deny that dependency, and it can lead us to be intolerant of the more obviously needy.

Grandiosity, the Greatest Danger

Intolerance of the weak and needy can find another expression besides outright rejection. It can come out in a compulsive, fix-it mentality. Yes, the weak and needy are welcome, but their lives *must* be turned around, quickly. We start playing God. Whether with radical measures to save a marriage, dramatic counseling techniques to rescue the emotionally disturbed, or high-pressure efforts to reform a sinning member, we may barge on, drunk with just enough success to be oblivious to our error.

Unfortunately, many churches and church communities who have focused on "healing ministries" have eventually had to deal with the fallout of over-intervention: burnout on the part of those ministering, the overuse of authority, people who are more hurt than helped. David's words in Psalm 131 can guide us to a more modest outlook:

> O Lord, my heart is not proud, or my eyes
>   haughty;
> Nor do I involve myself in great matters,
> Or in things too difficult for me.
> Surely I have composed and quieted my soul;
> Like a weaned child rests against his mother,
> My soul is like a weaned child within me.
> O Israel, hope in the Lord
> From this time forth and forever (NASB).

Reba Place Church, struggling with the tendency to over-responsibility and over-intervention, has been trying to learn a more modest sense of responsibility and, with it, the patience to live with what they cannot change. A situation like Sarah's was helpful. Apart from God's miraculous intervention, Sarah would die within weeks. There was nothing they could do about that. They were not called to save her life, and only God could save her soul. Their mandates were more simple: to care for her for a limited time and to share the good news. God's love got to Sarah through the caregivers. How she responded was between her and the Lord.

Guidelines for Ministry

How can a church minister best to those who are needy without getting top-heavy?

1. Be sure those who feel their need are welcomed. Some of us don't realize our own neediness, and because of that we expect to be welcomed wherever we go. Not so with handicapped people. If we don't really want them in our midst, they'll soon know it. Welcoming them can be as basic as providing ramps for wheelchairs or sign language for the deaf.

Reba's ministry to many of the emotionally disturbed and retarded people began simply: a member who worked in the sheltered-care institution invited several residents to church. A ministry to Cambodian refugees began simply by sponsoring one family. A wife and mother in the congregation contributed many hours to helping this family get settled, and a student volunteer spent one summer full time establishing a relationship with the family members. When the family was invited to church, they came, and even though Reba's members could speak no Khmer and the refugees could speak very little English, they soon invited their friends, who invited their relatives, and on and on.

Soon 80 Cambodians were coming regularly to worship, and 43 adults were baptized and joined the church. After a few years this number shook down as several Cambodian families resettled in other parts of the United States closer to other relatives. But a retired man still devotes most of his time to Reba's Cambodian population; a handful of others have also given of themselves and their time over the long haul. The church didn't plan a ministry to Cambodians; they came and stayed because individual members made them feel welcome.

2. Share the task. Any difficult ministry will fizzle and the person trying to carry it will burn out if the burden is not shared with others.

3. Create a community. Part of sharing the task is to make sure the church really functions like the body of Christ. People need to support one another, know their different gifts, and be free to use them. This comes from being together.

One night a Reba member was awakened at 3:30 a.m. by the doorbell. He opened the door to find a body sprawled on the steps. "Call the police!" he yelled to his wife. His first thought was that the woman was a rape victim. A great bruise was appearing on her bloated face. A moan assured him that she was still alive.

Then his wife said, "Look—it's Maggie!" He took another look. Maggie looked so bad he had not been able to recognize her. In a complete daze she began to try and get up. The couple helped her into the house.

Then they realized Maggie was drunk, totally stoned.

Maggie was an alcoholic. For years she had been part of Reba Place Church, and dry. Then she spent a year in Europe. When she returned, she avoided the church, and they couldn't really engage her.

But this night, as she staggered down the dark street, she knew help was available. When she fell and hit her face, she crawled to the door of the nearest church member. Because many in the church had moved into the same neighborhood around the meetinghouse to build a community environment, she could have gone to the six-flat next door, the family four doors down, or any of a dozen homes on nearby streets. Almost anyone who comes in contact with the church soon learns where members' homes are in the neighborhood, and they know they are welcome at any of them.

After resting on the couple's couch the rest of the night, the husband took Maggie home. A call to an elder who knew Maggie well put her back into contact with people she knew and trusted. Today with the assistance of AA, Maggie is dry again, and is renewing her relationship with the Lord and the church.

4. *Squander your resources.* Modern industry and business have taught people to be cost-effective. Do our efforts produce tangible returns? Sometimes in the church we, too, worry about that.

For example, for many years Reba Place had an all-church meal each Friday evening. Not all members came, but it was an enjoyable time of fellowship that enhanced their experience of community. However, more and more people from the Ridgeview Sheltered Care Home began coming. Some of these folks also came to worship, but there were several who only took advantage of the free meal. Word got around; a few homeless from Chicago began showing up regularly.

For them it was a chance to "go out" for an evening. They showed no interest in the Lord, they seemed uncouth to some observers, drinking up the coffee before others got their share, and spilling things without cleaning them up adequately.

Some church members were about to propose some method of restricting their participation or requiring something in return—even if it was just regular church attendance. But then they were reminded of Luke 14:12-14, where Jesus said, "When you give a luncheon or dinner, do not invite your friends, your brothers or relatives, or your rich neighbors; if you do, they may invite you back and so you will be repaid. But when you give a banquet, invite the poor, the crippled, the lame, the blind, and you will be blessed. Although they cannot repay you, you will be repaid at the resurrection of the righteous."

5. *Avoid being manipulated.* Dave Jackson recalls how the manipulations of one needy man led to a big fight between him and his wife, Neta.

The Jackson family was ready to leave for their monthly trip to the library when the phone rang. When Dave answered the phone, Bernie said he had to come over and talk immediately. Dave answered that there was no way he could talk right then.

"It could be very important to you and several other people," Bernie warned.

"Can you tell me briefly over the phone?"

"No. it's too serious to mention on the phone."

"I'm sorry," answered Dave. "I'm ready to walk out the door with my family."

"Where did you think that one up?" challenged Bernie. "How come you won't talk to me, Dave? Are you afraid of me?"

"No. You know I'm not afraid of you, Bernie."

Dave still says he wasn't afraid of Bernie, even though Bernie had punched him in the stomach once. But he was a very unstable character, had been frequently arrested and institutionalized. Sometimes he showed up at worship in shirt and tie; at other times disheveled and unshaven. And he could be genuinely frightening. Once he forcibly entered the house of his ex-wife, a Reba member, threatening and yelling.

Jackson did not want to take a chance that Bernie might show up at his house the next day while he was away at work. It was then that he buckled to the manipulation. Without thinking he promised to meet with Bernie the next evening at 7:30. Grudgingly, Bernie accepted the plan.

But when Dave told his wife, she got upset. Didn't he remember that he had agreed to take care of the kids the next evening so that she could go to practice for a special church program? Trying to talk to a nearly out-of-control Bernie while overseeing the kids just wouldn't work!

They argued all the way to the library. By this time the kids were upset, too. Dave knew Neta was right, but he felt trapped between his family and Bernie.

Finally, even though there was a chance that Bernie might

become more irrational if he canceled, Dave called him back and succeeded in rescheduling the appointment. Graciously, God calmed Bernie's anger, and he accepted a new plan.

6. *Be clear about sin.* Including sinners in our midst is sometimes confused with approving their sin. This shouldn't surprise us, since it happened frequently to Jesus. But we can and should do certain things to prevent misunderstandings, especially when something more than our reputations is at stake.

A couple years ago one of the families at Reba invited an unwed mother and her new baby to live with them for about six months until they could make more permanent arrangements. The young mother had repented of her sin and had received God's forgiveness. This was known and accepted by the adults in the church. The life the church family was able to provide Lisa and her new daughter had almost all the benefits of a normal home. There was physical care, hot meals, laundry, plenty of space, warm fellowship, support, and protection.

But the family's five-year-old daughter, who adored babies, watched everything carefully. Then one day she announced: "When I get big and have a baby, I don't think I'll get married."

Of course they had to talk about how important daddies were, and it gave them a nudge to be more deliberate in their teaching about God's plan for the family.

The Rewards of Ministry

The fear that too many needy people in our midst may weaken our faith in a God who transforms and restores is like Peter's fear of walking on water. We may be afraid to try because we don't want to face the possibility of sinking. On the other hand, if we don't try, we can be sure we won't be present when God does work in mighty ways.

Also, embracing those in need diffuses the horror of being

weak and needy. Maybe the most frightening aspect of personal need and tragedy is the prospect of having to face it alone. But when we welcome those in need, we underline the message that it is okay to have needs. We all have them, and we'll not forsake one another when they strike close to home. We're not God, so we can't fix everything, but we can stand by each other while God works his purpose out.

When five-year-old Rachel first saw Sarah Phillips, she asked anxiously about her ALS disease: "Will that ever happen to me?"

But a short time later Sarah was wheeled into Reba's worship service to feebly give her testimony of her new faith in Jesus and to be baptized. Rachel leaned over to her mother and said, "Now I don't feel so bad for Sarah, because I know she's going to see Jesus pretty soon."

And she was right. Within days Rachel's prediction came true.

Welcoming the weak and needy often stretches us beyond what we think we can give. But then we discover that there's truth in the children's song: "Love is something if you give it away . . . you'll end up having more."

For Group Discussion

1. Discuss how ambivalence can creep in when a ministry task looks like it will saddle us with ongoing service to weak or disturbed people. List three such situations. What should we do when we foresee that the needy are likely to remain needy for a long time?

2. Why might it be helpful to pay more attention to spiritual gifts than to who is or isn't needy when trying to include new people? What problems might result?

3. What does the presence of the weak and needy in our midst say about our faith or God's power to change? Is it important for the upbuilding of people's faith to experience success in spiritual power?

4. Wanting to fix everyone can appear to be great compassion, but in what ways can it signify a spiritual grandiosity? What might be some of the consequences for being compulsively driven to fix everyone?

CHAPTER THIRTEEN

Reaching Out in Corporate Witness

We are God's covenant people. In our local churches we gather, not as a group of individuals, but as the body of Christ. In worship (to God) and community (with one another) we are empowered through the Holy Spirit to go out, not as individuals, but as the body of Christ in mission (to the world). In all of these aspects we become witnesses to the power of God to forgive, redeem, renew, and make whole.

This vision of integration and wholeness in our mission must remain before us as the church moves into the last years of this century. We cannot let the highly specialized nature of our technological society continue to fragment us, isolating the "hand" from the "eye" and the "foot" of the body of Christ, thus diminishing the power of our witness.

Even as the year 2001 crowds upon us (and it used to be only a movie!), the basic needs of men and women have not changed in spite of space-age trappings. The world still needs to know—and that includes our neighbor next door—that no sin or failing can separate them from God's love, that they can be forgiven through Christ's redeeming work on the cross, that life in Christ is a new life, that God's people stand ready to welcome them with open arms, and that each one becomes an important part of witnessing to the kingdom of God in our midst: "What does the Lord require of you? To act justly and to love mercy and to walk humbly with your God" (Mic. 6:8).

Reaching Out in Mission

As we nurture this vision in our own church communities and seek ways to make it a reality, let's remember that even in an age of instant pictures, instant photocopies, and fast food restaurants, it still takes a seed time to grow, bud, and be harvested. Sometimes we will plant the seed, sometimes we will water it or nurture it along, sometimes reap the ripened bud that others have planted and watered.

Even more important is to keep clear what our role is and what is the role of the Holy Spirit. Kenneth C. Haugk says in *Christian Caregiving—A Way of Life*:

> The apostle Paul knew this. In 1 Cor. 3:6-7 he wrote, "I planted, Apollos watered, but God gave the growth. So neither he who plants nor he who waters is anything, but only God who gives the growth." As a farmer's responsibility rests with preparing a crop for harvest, so the Christian caregiver's responsibility is to "plant" and "water." God then provides the growth. In other words, *Christians are responsible for care; God is responsible for cure.*[1]

Understanding our role as *witnesses* to God's love and redemption, opening ourselves to be conduits of God's love to others, frees us from false expectations. Yes, we need to work hard to establish relationships, to reach out, to bring in, to share the gospel—but we must rely on the Holy Spirit for results.

Understandably, at some point we must ask, what can we do in our congregation? What have others done? How can we go about tilling the ground, planting the seed, or watering along the way that will give the Holy Spirit fertile ground in which to work?

Casting the Net

In the New Testament, witnesses were sometimes likened to "sowers of seed," or "fishers of men." In biblical times, seeds were not planted one by one, but were "sown"—that is, scattered broadly. And fishing was not done with a hook and line, but a large net was thrown out into the sea.

Using Telemarketing and Advertising

Harmony Christian Fellowship in Antioch, Tennessee, decided to throw a large net as they relocated from Goshen, Indiana, to the Nashville area. The core group of 12 adults and several children met in homes for a while, but decided they should have a new beginning.

"It's hard starting something new in a large metropolitan area," said Wayne Detweiler, copastor with his wife, Sue. But using telemarketing techniques implemented by other churches, they obtained a cross-reference directory (listings by street and area) and blanketed the Antioch area with phone calls. Their Partner in Mission church, North Leo Mennonite Church in Leo, Indiana, sent six people (mostly retired) to help make 20,000 phone calls during a four-week period.

When they called, they did not pretend to know the person or be overly friendly (as in: "Hi, Mr. Smith, how are you today?"). Instead, they introduced themselves, and asked for permission to ask a few questions ("Do you attend a local church?" etc.). "If they had a church," said Detweiler, "we encouraged them and said good-bye. If they didn't have one, we asked if we could send them our literature." Finally the person was invited to Opening Sunday, December 6, 1987.

On Opening Sunday, 130 persons were in attendance, many of whom stayed afterward to talk over coffee and cookies. One woman said, "You know, I haven't been to church in 16 years. Then you called, and you kept sending me mail. Then you called again ... and I knew in my heart that it was time to come. I'm glad I did; I believe it was really the Lord who called me."

Another woman with a young child came to Harmony as a result of the phone call after not attending anywhere for 11 years. "I want my child to grow up in church. I couldn't wait any longer." The next Sunday, to her surprise, her husband came, too.

A month later Harmony Christian Fellowship was averaging 50 each Sunday—a nearly 300 percent increase. It was their new beginning—and a new beginning for the people who entered a church for the first time in years, as well.

Downey Mennonite Church, Downey, California, also used telemarketing techniques to revitalize their small (25-30 old-line Mennonite members) church. In the fall of 1986, Ron Grosser, a pastor with a vision for evangelism and church growth, rented half a dozen phones from the telephone company, and using the Downey telephone directory called *thousands* of people, telling them a little bit about the church, and inviting them to a Celebration Sunday on Easter 1987.

In the meantime, Downey Mennonite Church became *Living Hope Church of Downey*—a name change meant to broaden their image as a *community* church. Grosser also went immediately to two services—one for younger attenders interested in church renewal and praise services; the other aimed more toward traditional (and older) members.

The results? The first campaign resulted in 75 total attenders (15 of whom became members).

Living Hope recently added a second pastor and launched a second telemarketing campaign in the fall of 1987. Out of approximately 10,000 phone calls, 2,000 people requested brochures on the church. On the second Celebration Sunday in November 1987, 156 people were in attendance.

The two pastors continue to call people back. Glenn Koons, the new associate pastor, said he made at least 200 call-backs in one week alone. And on New Year's Eve, 21 more people joined the church. As 1988 began, average attendance at Living Hope was 110, of whom 75 were members—all since the fall of 1986, just a little more than a year.

Koons says that the way to keep these new attenders coming is to involve them in home Bible studies (similar to kinship groups). Those interested in membership also go through a new members class conducted by the pastor for several weeks. "We are not growing because we are a Mennonite Church," says Koons, "but because we're using church growth principles." However, during the new members class the Mennonite Brethren confession is used as the basis of discipleship, and Living Hope strongly affirms their Anabaptist roots and teachings.

Cape Christian Fellowship uses the media in other ways to "cast the net." Dennis and Linda Gingerich moved to Cape Coral, Florida, in May 1986 to join two other couples in planting a church. They concentrated on building a core group for the first year, which grew to around 35 adults and children.

This congregation picked Easter Sunday 1987 as the beginning date of the new church. A few weeks before Easter they mailed an announcement to 16,000 homes, inviting people to that first Easter service. Sixty persons responded to the mail campaign that first Sunday ... and people are still coming from time to time seven to nine months later as a result of the initial mailing.

As follow-up, the church included a brochure about the church in a community-sponsored "coupon packet" (just one of several advertising pieces in the packet) that went to 10,000 homes at a cost of 6¢ per household. This mailing brought several visitors, and two or three families began coming regularly as a result of that brochure. Attendance gradually grew to around 70 to 85 persons each Sunday by early January 1988.

Cape Christian keeps their eyes open for ways to cast the net. Dennis coaches a local soccer team for boys 9-11 years of age. The church agreed to be the team sponsor (just like Bill's Service Station and First Federal Bank). The team shirts have the name of the church on them, and the church gets advertising space on the playing field billboards. When the team plays, often people ask about the church. Several families whose boys play on the team were curious about the team's sponsor and started coming to the church.

A Community Survey

Another means of casting the net is to conduct a community religious survey. Every house or apartment in your church neighborhood is visited by some member of your congregation during a stated period (perhaps a week). In an area with many churches the project might be done in cooperation with other interested Christian churches in the area. If each denomination conducts a separate census, the multitude of census takers threatens to become a neighborhood nuisance. When churches work together, the results can be shared and each church assume responsibility for those whom their program seems most likely to reach.

• Two for Twenty

The area should be divided into sections small enough for a team of visitors to cover, perhaps twenty families to a team. Going two-by-two as Jesus sent his disciples is a good model to follow. Information should be recorded on cards, a separate card for each household. On the card list the family name, the address, and information about each person in the household: (1) name, (2) age, (3) church membership, attendance, or preference. If no one is at home or the family refuses to give information, this fact should be recorded instead.

• *Assigning Responsibility*

As the result of this census your congregation can make up a responsibility list of unchurched people whom you should try to visit and invite. Each person on this list can be assigned as a special responsibility to a church group, either the Sunday school class to which this person would belong if he or she came to your church, or a special interest group (choirs, youth, single parents' support group, men's or women's fellowships) whose activities would be most likely to appeal to this person.

The chances are that your list will become too long to be realistic. Pray for the Holy Spirit's guidance to show you how to proceed. You may need to revise your list to include only those whom each group will be most likely to reach because of similarity in age, sex, occupation, or secular interests.

• *Deciding Your Purpose*

Once your group receives a reasonable list of persons to visit, decide whether the first visit is to be just a friendly call which will open the way for later visits and an invitation to fellowship in the church. Or, on the first visit, you may want to invite the person or family to a specific group activity. Either way, it's helpful to have literature to leave in the home when you call: a brochure about your church fellowship, or a flyer about a special activity.

• *Preparing the Group to Visit*

Meet together first for worship, prayer, and planning. Pray especially for the persons on your list and for guidance in planning an approach. It may be best for the group to go out two by two. (A larger visiting team is likely to cause the person visited to feel that he or she is outnumbered and about to be outtalked.) Work out all the practical details of transportation, dates for the visitation to be completed, and so forth.

In planning for visitation, consider the time which will be most convenient for the persons you expect to visit. This will differ from community to community, but usually parents at home prefer visits on weekday afternoons before the children come home from school. Working people may have more time to talk on weekday evenings or weekends. Students are likely to feel most relaxed on Friday nights.

• *Pointers for Successful Visits:*
    1. Before calling, think and pray about subjects for conversation. If the persons are strangers to you, try to find out beforehand something about their occupation, their interests, or your mutual friends so that you have something to talk about.
    2. Identify yourself immediately if you are not known to the family. If they already know you, tell them why you called. "We're representing the adult Sunday school class of the First Christian Church. Our group is out tonight trying to get better acquainted with our neighbors," will keep your host from wondering, "What under the shining sun made these people decide to call?"
    3. If you have called at a time that is obviously inconvenient, leave quickly with the offer to come again when there is more time to talk. Even the most charming visitor will not meet a sincerely enthusiastic welcome from a student cramming for next day's examination, a person doing last-minute figuring on income tax, a parent putting children to bed, or a family about to go away.

• *Readiness to Witness*
    If an opportunity presents itself, visitors should be ready to share the good news of the gospel or respond to a need for prayer, but only as a natural outgrowth of the conversation, not

forced into it. The visit is not designed primarily for personal evangelism but to begin a redemptive friendship which will draw new friends into the influence of your Christian group.

• *Sharing Prayers and Testimonies*

After the visits have been completed, gather together in your group for sharing experiences and for prayer and thanksgiving. If the visitation is an all-out effort by all the adult and youth groups of your congregation, the project can be worked out in connection with the congregational midweek prayer meeting— meeting together for prayer before you go out, and then coming back together to share and pray.

What Are Your Resources?

Whether or not you do a community survey, followed by a visitation, understand your resources for evangelism within your own congregation. List the fellowship groups which already exist in your congregation. Adult and youth Sunday school classes will probably head the list. Write each one down separately by name or the age-group it includes. Then add youth groups, missionary auxiliary, service groups, men's or women's fellowships, home Bible studies, choirs, and any other organizations.

Every one of these groups, imperfect as they are, have evangelistic potential. Likely many persons in these groups would like to be more evangelistic but don't quite know how. A Christian high-school student, for instance, felt guilty because she lacked the courage to talk about Christ to her popular and very secular classmates. At the same time there was a friendless, foreign-born girl in her class whose odd ways and quick temper antagonized others. Unfortunately the Christian girl did not recognize the real opportunity for evangelism—to befriend the stranger and draw her into a circle of Christian friends.

Many Christian young people and older ones, too, pass by similar opportunities because they do not understand the drawing power of Christian fellowship. Think of the enlarged witness if each group you have listed would draw into its circle just one person who does not know Christ.

Each group wishing to extend its evangelizing fellowship should consider the following:

• *Examine the quality of your group life.* The questions on discipleship in Chapter 8 for both individuals and the group as a whole could be the basis for a profitable discussion.

• *Encourage one another to cultivate friendship with an unsaved person of your acquaintance.* Christians alert for opportunities to build friendship will find many occasions to extend kindness to those they contact at work, in the neighborhood, or at school. Friendship must, of course, be offered sincerely. It cannot be a mask put on just long enough to trick another person into coming to your meeting.

• *Invite this person to share fellowship with your group.* Build your relationship until it seems quite natural to say, "Our singles Sunday school class is having a skating party on Friday night. Why don't you go along with me?" Or, "Saturday evening our choir is going to sing carols for some of the older folks in town. We could use another good tenor. Won't you help us out?"

• *Brush up on your welcome.* The response of the group to each visitor is crucial. There is no excuse for cliquishness in a group of believers. It is especially disastrous when displayed toward those who are beginning to show some hunger for Christian fellowship. Only when outsiders discover that Christians in a group are just as friendly and interested as the individual believers they have learned to know will the barriers begin to break down.

• *Consider the advantages of an indirect approach.* A person who has never shown interest in coming to church will more readily accept· an invitation to a group activity from a classmate, neighbor, or fellow worker with whom he or she has already had some good times than from a stranger calling as part of a church visiting team. After this first introduction to the group, it will be less difficult to ask the friend to participate in other activities or attend worship. Newcomers who are made to feel at home will want to come back.

• *Keep in mind your ultimate ·goal.* Eventually, of course, each new person in your fellowship must come face to face with the claims of Christ. Only rarely does this happen alone through the general influence of group association. More often the group experience whets the unsaved person's hunger to hear and know more about the reality which these Christian friends have found. Fellowship is not a substitute for, but a powerful aid to, other forms of evangelism, such as one-to-one witnessing, Christian education, and preaching. The evangelistic situation, however, should not be forced. Only the Holy Spirit knows when a person is ready to decide. Allow the Spirit to lead you in the Spirit's own time.

Reaching Out to Specific People Groups

Even though every congregation has evangelizing potential in the groups that already exist, many needs in your community may not be addressed by the program you have to offer. Depending on the area in which your church is located—urban, suburban, rural; low-income, high-income; homes, apartments; elderly residents, working couples, families—casting your net may mean being sensitive to the needs of the people around you.

Jesus did this. He healed the blind and the lame; he befriended a despised and lonely tax-collector; he welcomed children. He began at the point of need and shared his love.

If we are truly interested in sharing Christ's love and re-demption with those around us, we, too, need to begin at the point of their need and minister to them in the name of Christ.

Reach Out to Families

Families are under a lot of stress today. Working parents and single parent families often find it all they can handle to manage work and basic family needs. They may have little time or energy left over to consider church or midweek activities, which seem like just another obligation.

Too many churches tend to divide people into overly sim-plistic categories—such as unmarrieds and marrieds, or parents and nonparents, or young and old. Ministry tends to be focused around counseling with individuals or families who are not cop-ing with the normal demands of life.

Dr. Dennis B. Guernsey, associate professor and director of Marriage and Family Ministries at Fuller Theological Sem-inary, suggests that "family ministry in the church can be struc-tured in such a way that it understands and uses the life cycle of the family as an organizing principle around which it provides preventive education and support."[2] Guernsey defines these family life stages as follows:

1. The between-families young adult.
2. The newly married young adults.
3. Families with their first child/preschool children.
4. Families with middle years children.
5. Families with teens.
6. Parents with an empty nest.
7. The retirement/elderly years.
8. The adult single person and single parents.[3]

Says Guernsey, "No other institution has stepped forward to educate or support the family during these transitions. This vacuum provides the church with its moment of opportunity with families. Families need real help and support at these predictable times and in ways that are known and available."[4] Some Christian publishers are realizing this need and are providing materials to help churches reach out to families in various life stages.[5]

As the result of a community survey in 1965, Reba Place Church discovered that the most pressing need in their area of Evanston, Illinois, was for day-care for working and single parents. Reba Place Day Nursery has provided nursery school and day-care for white, black, Hispanic, and Asian children for more than twenty years. Lois Shuford, the present director, was not a Christian when she brought her five-year-old daughter, Becky, to RPDN. But through the loving care of the staff, she and her husband, Bob, accepted Christ, were baptized the next year, and have been members at Reba ever since.

Maple Grove Mennonite Church, in Atglen, Pennsylvania, developed a LIFT program to meet the needs of mothers at home with young children. Child care is provided at the church one morning a week while the mothers attend a LIFT program geared to their interests and needs. The response was so great that a preschool grew around the LIFT program which meets four mornings a week. LIFT (which is free) currently serves 90 mothers and 90 children; 88 families are enrolled in the preschool (which charges tuition). Both programs bring mothers from the church and community together.

A similar program is MOPS (Mothers of Preschoolers).[6] James Dobson calls this "one of the best forms of family *outreach* I've seen.... Talk about meeting real needs! Mothers love this program and will come even if they have no interest in or knowledge of the church. Then, if the program is conducted properly, they usually begin attending the Sunday services."[7]

Other family outreach programs include *Latchkey*, which

provides after-school care for children whose parents work, and *Family Nights* at church, when there are activities (Bible study, youth groups, crafts for kids, etc.) for all age-groups, so families can come together rather than go different ways on different nights.

Reach Out to Youth

Tom and Claire Osinkosky moved to Peace Mennonite Fellowship in Grande Prairie, Alberta, with their eight children to help rebuild a dying church. Because there were only two families to begin with, they looked for a youth group in another church for their three teens—but none of the surrounding churches had a teen group!

The Osinkoskys realized a program for area teens was a neglected opportunity. So in April 1987 they opened a coffeehouse in the basement of their little church. They had two goals: fellowship for Christian kids, and a means of evangelism.

The coffeehouse is called THE DEN. The young man who suggested the name says, "A fox raises its young in a den until they are ready to go out on their own; it is a place of nurture." The Den is a gathering place each weekend for 100-125 kids from all denominations. It supposedly is for teens up to age 16—but the 18-to-23-year-olds come, too. This latter group is most likely to also attend Sunday services at Peace Mennonite.

From 50 to 60 people are attending Peace Mennonite now, just a year later, and about 20 of those are teens. Two teens have recommitted their lives to the Lord. The Den was also responsible for bringing one family into the church.

In Evanston, Illinois, director Mike Murphy was grateful for the successful Young Life program (a national parachurch ministry) which was reaching kids for Christ in the local high schools. But he realized that there was a growing need to be reaching junior high kids. At the same time, several local

Evanston churches were struggling with the lack of a youth ministry for their own junior high age kids. A partnership was proposed between Young Life and the local churches, and CONTACT was born. The youth from the different churches come together twice a month for activities and club nights, providing grateful churches and parents with a program for their own youth which they could not provide alone, and something for the church youth to bring their school friends to. After only six months, CONTACT was averaging 80 junior high kids from different denominations and unchurched.

A number of unchurched kids who go with their friends to CONTACT on Friday night also began attending Sunday school. One Sunday morning during sharing time a 12-year-old girl from a non-Christian family came up to the front (accompanied by three other giggling supporters) and thanked her Sunday school teachers and CONTACT leaders "for giving us kids such wonderful things to do."

Bahia Vista, a church in Sarasota, Florida, realized that *one* program would not meet the different levels of commitment represented among their teens. Laban Miller, the minister of youth, discovered they needed (1) an outreach level (for non-Christian kids); (2) a growth level (for Christian kids needing to grow); and (3) a ministry level (for mature Christian kids wanting to grow through helping others grow).

Bahia Vista set up a program to help meet the needs at all three levels. There is an outreach event two times a month; Sunday morning is aimed at growth level kids; and a teen ministry team meets monthly to plan for and share responsibility for the other teen events.

Reach Out to Those in Crisis

A number of churches are realizing that the church should be at the forefront of responding to those in crisis. Are we giving "a cup of cold water" in Christ's name? Or are we letting secular agencies respond to pressing needs while we sit idly by and wonder why the gospel seems irrelevant to society around us?

Washington Community Fellowship, in Washington, D.C., translated its concern about abortion into concern for the pregnant women in crisis. In cooperation with other D.C. churches and under the umbrella of the Christian Action Council (a nondenominational ministry), WCF helps sponsor and staff a Crisis Pregnancy Center which provides pregnancy tests, spiritual counseling, and support to over 550 persons (including some friends, relatives, and boyfriends) per year. Lynn Marry, the director and a member at WCF, says about half the women they see are leaning toward abortion or are undecided. Of those, about 64 percent choose to carry their babies to term. The other half lean toward keeping their babies, but need support and counseling to get through the difficult days ahead.

The Christian Action Council encourages churches to also provide Shepherding Homes, where a young woman with a crisis pregnancy can live temporarily until she has her baby and gets back on her feet. This program seems to be more needed and more successful in some communities than others. One Chicago church who has welcomed several pregnant young women (usually referred by relatives) has also seen these women renew their relationship with Christ. And three have found Christian husbands and established Christian homes in the midst of the church family!

Diamond Street Mennonite Church is located in one of the poorest sections of Philadelphia. A few years ago people in the community came to them and asked if they would help save a four-story building nearby which was going to be torn down. They thought it might be used for various community projects and services. As a result, a group was formed of both church and community people called Diamond Street Community Center, which purchased the building.

Diamond Street Mennonite was outgrowing their church property. Instead of building, they moved into the Community Center, and put their "building fund" into renovating it. All this coincided with the church's desire to spend more of itself in mission and ministry. They decided on a Holistic Health Center which would seek to minister to the whole person: physical needs, spiritual needs, social needs. Three doctors and a counselor serve on a volunteer basis. Most of the staff are volunteers, though the center does hire a few people—a custodian, a nurse, a secretary.

The Holistic Health Center ministers to anyone regardless of financial need, using a sliding fee scale, Fees pay only a fraction of the center's budget, which is over $100,000 a year. Other costs are covered by contributions from local businesses, individuals, and groups.

The LaSalle Street Church, in Chicago, provides a weekly breakfast for the elderly poor in its church neighborhood. This is only one of a wide variety of ministries they provide for specific people groups in their area of the city. The people around LaSalle know that the church doors are open for them seven days a week.

Reach Out Beyond Your Church

Many churches of all denominations give to missions, or support missionaries. But some churches are realizing the value of participating in missions themselves.

In January 1986, Neffsville Mennonite Church near Lancaster, Pennsylvania, sent its first team of 17 persons to Haiti to build two church buildings. One year later a team of nine went to Port-au-Prince, Haiti, for two weeks under a similar program. Then through Mennonite Central Committee's SWAP program (Sharing With Appalachian People), Neffsville sent a group of about 30 persons to Harlan, Kentucky, for two successive summers. The team members ranged from 6 to 60 years of age.

Terry Yoder, the assistant pastor at Neffsville, said he appreciated the Kentucky experience in particular. The team worked through the day. In the evening they had a chance to talk together and integrate their experience. They discussed the poverty and the history and nature of Harlan County. The modernization of mining has left many people jobless, but they don't want to move away because this is where their family is. "Hopefully we were able to serve the people in Kentucky," said Yoder, "but I'm especially excited to see the impact of this experience on our young people's lifestyle and stewardship."

Reaching out beyond our church in friendship by sponsoring an Asian refugee family, or participating in the Overground Railroad which tries to help Central American refugees find a home in Canada with assistance from various churches along the way, may not be "evangelism" per se. But giving a "cup of cold water" to others beyond the boundaries of our church can definitely plant or water the seeds of faith if we do it in Christ's name.

In so doing we may capture a new vision for mission: the body of Christ worshiping, living, working hand in hand to share the good news of the kingdom of God.

Gathered for Power[8]

By Neta Jackson

I was glad
When they said to me,
"Let us go into the house of the Lord!"

What makes this
God's house?
Simply that we are gathered
   the hands
   the feet
   the tongue
   the eyes
   the ears
   the knees
of the body of Christ
brought together into our
wholeness.

Alone
     we are each God's children.
Together
     we are his body.
Gathered
     there is power for praise . . .
         . . . encouragement
         . . . witness
         . . . hope.

For Group Discussion

1. The image of casting the net broadly is offered to describe what some might call "impersonal" forms of witness. What do you think of these methods? How do you understand them in relation to the ways Jesus cast the net broadly through public preaching to thousands?

2. What are some of the factors that might enter into your deciding what the purpose of an initial visit would be in following up on a survey?

3. The chapter suggests three pointers for successful visits. Discuss them and consider whether there are any others you think would be essential.

4. If we are truly interested in sharing Christ's love and redemption with those around us, it is important to begin at the point of their need and minister to them in the name of Christ. Review and discuss some of the most common points of need people have today. For each need, what is one specific way to respond?

Bibliography

Aldrich, Joseph, *Lifestyle Evangelism: Crossing Traditional Boundaries to Reach the Unbelieving World* (Portland, Oreg.: Multnomah Press, 1981).

Allen, Roland, *The Spontaneous Expansion of the Church* (London: World Dominion Press, 1960).

Arn, Win and Charles, *The Master's Plan for Making Disciples* (Pasadena: Church Growth Press, 1982).

Bontrager, G. Edwin, and Nathan D. Showalter, *It Can Happen Today!* and accompanying teacher's manual (Scottdale, Pa., Herald Press, 1986).

Coleman, Robert, *The Master Plan of Evangelism* (Old Tappan, N.J.: Fleming H. Revell, 1963).

——————, *The Master Plan of Discipleship* (Old Tappan, N.J.: Fleming H. Revell Co., 1987).

Eisenman, Tom, *Everyday Evangelism—Making the Most of Life's Common Moments* (Downers Grove, Ill.: InterVarsity Press, 1987).

Foster, Richard J., *Celebration of Dicsipline* (San Francisco: Harper and Row, Publishers, 1978).

Griffin, Em, *Getting Together* (Downers Grove, Ill.: InterVarsity Press, 1982).

Griswold, Roland E., *By Hook and Crook* (Charlotte, N.C.: Advent Christian General Conference, 1981).

Handy, Robert T., *Members One of Another* (Philadelphia: Judson Press, 1959).

Haugk, Kenneth C., *Christian Caregiving—A Way of Life* (Minneapolis: Augsburg Publishing House, 1984).

Hershberger, Guy F., *The Recovery of the Anabaptist Vision* (Scottdale, Pa.: Herald Press, 1957).

Jackson, Dave and Neta, *Glimpses of Glory: The Story of Reba Place Fellowship* (Elgin, Ill.: The Brethren Press, 1987).

Miller, Paul M., *Group Dynamics in Evangelism* (Scottdale, Pa.: Herald Press, 1958).

Pippert, Rebecca Manley, *Out of the Salt Shaker and into the World* (Downers Grove, Ill.: InterVarsity, 1979).

Raines, Robert A., *New Life in the Church* (San Francisco: Harper & Row Publishers, Inc., 1961).

Stedman, Ray C., *Body Life* (Ventura, Calif.: Regal Books, 1972).

Van Braght, Thieleman J., *Martyrs Mirror* (Scottdale, Pa.: [1660] 1950).

Wagner, C. Peter, *Leading Your Church to Growth* (Ventura, Calif.: Regal Books, 1984).

_____, *Your Church Can Grow* (Ventura, Calif.: Regal Books, [1976] 1985).

_____, *Your Spiritual Gifts Can Help Your Church Grow* (Ventura, Calif.: Gospel Light, 1979).

Webber, George W., *God's Colony in Man's World* (Nashville: Abingdon Press, 1960).

Webber, Robert, *Common Roots* (Grand Rapids, Mich.: Zondervan, 1978).

Ministry Resources
for Family Life Stages

The following are available from your local Christian bookstore or David C. Cook Publishing Co., 850 N. Grove Ave., Elgin, IL 60120. Each has thirteen sessions, with overhead transparencies and reproducible resource sheets.

On My Own—A Course for Young Singles, by Tom Eisenman, 1985.

Newly Married—A Course to Build Foundations, by Wayne Rickerson, 1985.

Now We Are Three—A Course for Parents-to-Be and New Parents, by Eldon Fry, George Rekers, and Judson Swihart, 1985.

Big People, Little People—A Course for Parents of Young Children, by Tom Eisenman, 1985.

You and Your Teen—A Course for Mid-Life Parents, by Charles Bradshaw, 1985.

Empty Nest—Life After the Kids Leave Home, by Earl D. Wilson, 1986.

The Freedom Years—A Celebration of Retirement, by Larry Ferguson with Dave Jackson, 1985.

Just Me and the Kids—A Course for Single Parents, by Patricia Brandt and Dave Jackson, 1985.

Notes

Chapter 1

1. Carl F. George, "A Tilt Toward the Relational," *Christianity Today*, Jan. 17, 1986, pp. 22-I,23-I.

2. Dave Jackson, "Strong Families," *The Christian Family Growing Together*, Fall 1985, p. 6.

3. Dave Jackson, "Power to Change Whom?" *Sunday Digest*, May 11, 1986, p. 6. Used by permission of the author.

4. Kevin Springer, "Four Characteristics of Growing Churches," *Commonlife*, Vol. 5, No. 4, pp. 6-9.

Chapter 2

1. Tom Eisenman, *Everyday Evangelism* (Downers Grove, Ill.: Inter-Varsity Press, 1987), p. 34.

2. Robert E. Coleman, "Every-Member Ministry," *Pastoral Renewal*, Vol. 12, No. 4, Nov. 1987, p. 3.

3. Stephen Board, "Wide-Funnel Churches: A New Trend?" *Innovations*, Summer 1985, p. 34.

4. Tom Allan, *The Face of My Parish* (New York: Harper and Row, 1957), p. 43.

5. Kenneth S. Kantzer, "The Priorities of Love," *Christianity Today*, Jan. 17, 1986, p. 30-I.

6. Ibid., Eisenman, p. 34.

Chapter 3

1. Robert Coleman, "Every-Member Ministry," *Pastoral Renewal*, Nov. 1987, Vol. 12, No. 4.

2. "Listening Without Communication Blocks," *Innovations for the Church Leader*, Summer 1984 (Elgin, Ill.: David C. Cook Publishing Co.), p. 24.

3. Marjorie Medary, *Each One Teach One* (New York: Longmans, Green and Co., 1954), pp. 31-32.

4. Ibid., p. 34.

5. Ibid., p. 41.

6. Carl Wesselhoeft, "Leading the Muslim in Worship," *Missionary Messenger*, Feb. 1960, pp. 3-4.

7. Bertha Swarr, "Israel Mission," *Gospel Herald*, Dec. 22, 1959, p. 1089.

Chapter 4

1. Ray C. Stedman, *Body Life* (Ventura, Calif.: Regal Books, 1972), p. 81.

2. J. Berkley Reynolds, "Lay Evangelism That Works," *Innovations*, Vol. 1, No. 4, Spring 1985, p. 28.

3. Roland Allen, *The Spontaneous Expansion of the Church* (London: World Dominion Press, 1960), p. 7.

4. Paul E. Little, "Lost Audience," *Christian Living*, Mar. 1960, p. 16.

5. Guy F. Hershberger, *The Recovery of the Anabaptist Vision* (Scottdale, Pa.: Herald Press, 1957), pp. 161-162.

6. Thieleman J. van Braght, *Martyrs Mirror* (Scottdale, Pa.: [1660] 1950), p. 894.

7. Ibid., p. 893.

8. Ibid., p. 481.

9. Ibid., p. 484.

10. Ibid., p. 515.

11. Ibid., p. 423.

12. Robert A. Raines, *New Life in the Church* (San Francisco: Harper & Row Publishers, Inc., 1961), p. 130.

13. C. Peter Wagner, *Your Spiritual Gifts* (Ventura, Calif.: Gospel Light, 1979), p. 42.

14. Ibid., p. 91.

Chapter 5

1. Richard J. Foster, *Celebration of Discipline* (San Francisco: Harper and Row, Publishers, 1978), pp. 138, 148.

2. Thieleman J. van Braght, *Martyrs Mirror* (Scottdale, Pa.: [1660] 1950), p. 414.

3. Paul F. W. Busing, "Reminiscences of Finkenwalde," *The Christian Century*, Sept. 20, 1961, p. 1110.

4. J. C. Macaulay, *A Devotional Commentary on the Acts of the Apostles* (Grand Rapids: William B. Eerdmans Publishing Co., 1946), p. 39.

Chapter 6

1. Dave and Neta Jackson, "Meg's Story," in *Glimpses of Glory* (Elgin, Ill.: The Brethren Press, 1987), p. 185-186.

2. David Wells, "How to Avoid Offensive Language While Saying Absolutely Nothing," *Christianity Today*, Jan. 15, 1988, p. 25.

3. Robert Webber, *Common Roots* (Grand Rapids, Mich.: Zondervan, 1978).

4. George W. Webber, *God's Colony in Man's World* (Nashville: Abingdon Press, 1960), pp. 53-54.

Chapter 7

1. James C. Bland, "How to Close the Back Door," *Christianity Today*, Vol. 30, No. 1, Jan. 17, 1986, p. 74.

2. Ibid.

3. Ray C. Stedman, *Body Life* (Ventura, Calif.: Regal Books, 1972, p. 2.

4. C. Peter Wagner, *Leading Your Church to Growth* (Ventura, Calif.: Regal Books, 1984), p. 23.

5. Roland E. Griswold, *By Hook and Crook* (Charlotte, N.C.: Advent Christian General Conference, 1981), p. 140.

6. C. Peter Wagner, *Your Church Can Grow* (Ventura, Calif.: Regal Books, [1976] 1985), p. 102.

7. Ibid., Wagner, *Leading Your Church to Growth*, pp. 58-59.

8. Ibid., pp. 59-60.

9. Ibid., Wagner, *Your Church Can Grow*, p. 111.

10. Ibid., p. 124.

11. Ibid., p. 136.

12. Dave and Neta Jackson, "Where Have All the Refugees Gone?" *Christian Herald*, Vol. 110, No. 9, Oct. 1987, p. 24.

Chapter 8

1. *Concern #8* (Scottdale, Pa., May 1960), pp. 41-42.

2. Ibid.

3. Tom Allan, *The Face of My Parish*, pp. 49-50.

4. Dietrich Bonhoeffer, *Life Together*, pp. 37, 38.

Chapter 9

1. Quoted by David W. Shenk, "New York City—But Mostly People," *Youth's Christian Companion*, Nov. 5, 1961, p. 714.

2. Em Griffin, *Getting Together* (Downers Grove, Ill.: InterVarsity Press, 1982), pp. 21-22.

3. Paul M. Miller, *Group Dynamics in Evangelism*, p. 19.

4. Ibid., p. 175.

5. David A. Womack, "Five Small-Group Myths," *Leadership*, Vol. VII, No. 1, Winter 1986, p. 118.

6. Rebecca Manley Pippert, *Out of the Salt Shaker and into the World* (Downers Grove, Ill.: InterVarsity, 1979), p. 170.

7. Paul Smith, "Life Cycle," *Small Group Series #6* (Kansas City, Mo.: Broadway Baptist Church, 1987). Adapted and used by permission of Paul Smith.

8. John Howard Yoder, "Christian Missions at the End of an Era," *Christian Living*, August 1961, pp. 14-15.

9. Roland E. Griswold, *By Hook and Crook* (Charlotte, N.C.: Advent Christian General Conference of America, Inc., 1981), p. 111.

10. Robert T. Handy, *Members One of Another* p. 56.

Chapter 10

1. Kevin M. Thompson, *Equipping the Saints* (Minneapolis: Christians in Action, 1981), p. 2.

2. C. Peter Wagner, *Your Spiritual Gifts Can Help Your Church Grow* (Ventura, Calif.: Regal Books, 1979), p. 39.

Chapter 11

1. "Keys to a Family-Friendly Church," *Leadership*, Winter 1986, Vol. VII, No. 1, p. 19.

2. Tom L. Eisenman, *Everyday Evangelism—Making the Most of Life's Common Moments* (Downers Grove, Ill.: InterVarsity Press, 1987), p. 14.

3. Ibid. Used by permission.

4. Robert Coleman, *The Master Plan of Discipleship* (Old Tappan, N.J.: Fleming H. Revell Co., 1987).

5. Eisenman, p. 127. Used by permission.

6. Joseph Aldrich, "Lifestyle Evangelism," in *Christianity Today*, Jan. 7, 1983.

7. Paul E. Little, "Lost Audience," *Christian Living*, Mar. 1960, p. 36.

8. Virgil Brenneman, "Sharing Easter with Many Lands at Home," *Gospel Herald*, June 7, 1960, p. 508.

9. Sidebar from "No Place for the Single Parent?" in *Moody Monthly*, October 1987.

10. Ibid.

11. Ibid.

12. Ibid.

13. Mrs. Alton Horst, "The Lamp of Community Witness," *Gospel Herald*, Mar. 7, 1961, p. 202.

Chapter 12

1. Adapted from: Dave Jackson, "Bacteria in the Body," *Leadership*, Vol. IV, No. 1, Winter 1983, pp. 65-71. Used by permission of the author.

Chapter 13

1. Kenneth C. Haugk, *Christian Caregiving—A Way of Life* (Minneapolis: Augsburg Publishing House, 1984), p.19.

2. Dennis B. Guernsey, "The Church and the Life Stages of Its Families," *Innovations*, Bonus Issue 1985, p. 10.

3. These two groups of people are not technically stages, but have their own needs which need creative responses from the church.

4. Guernsey, *Innovations*, Bonus Issue 1985, p. 8.

5. See Ministry Resources for Family Life Stages in the Bibliography.

6. More information is available from MOPS Outreach, Inc., 2269 W. Yale, Englewood, CO 80110.

7. An Interview with James Dobson, "Keys to a Family-Friendly Church," *Leadership*, Winter 1986, Vol. VII, No. 1, p. 14.

8. Neta Jackson, ©1983. Used by permission.

Authors

A. Grace Wenger retired after 39 years of teaching which took her from a one-room school near New Holland, Pennsylvania, to the Northeast Institute of Technology in the People's Republic of China. Twenty-two of those years were in Mennonite schools, Eastern Mennonite High School and Lancaster Mennonite High School. For thirteen years she taught at Millersville University, where her special interest in teaching English as a second language and a second dialect won statewide recognition.

Born near Lancaster, Pennsylvania, she earned her bachelor's degree at Elizabethtown College and her master's degree at the University of Pennsylvania. She has written Sunday school curriculum materials and mission study books for Herald Press. Presently she is writing the history of her home congregation, Groffdale Mennonite, which dates back to 1717.

Dave and Neta Jackson are full-time writers and editors who specialize in coauthoring books with others. They are the parents of two children, Julian (1969) and Rachel (1975), and have been members of Reba Place Fellowship in Evanston, Illinois, since 1973.

Dave was born in Glendale, California, the son of parents involved in rural church planting. He graduated from Multnomah School of the Bible, then from Judson College with a degree in journalism, and did graduate work in communications at Wheaton College. For eight years Dave was a pastoral elder at Reba Place Fellowship, teaching and leading both a small group and an extended family household before returning full time to editing and writing.

Neta was born in Winchester, Kentucky, to parents involved in Christian schools as teachers and administrators. Family moves soon took them to Seattle, Washington, where she grew up on the campus of King's Garden, a nondenominational Christian ministry center. Neta attended Multnomah School of the Bible for one year, where she met Dave, then graduated from Wheaton College with a B.A. in Literature. At Reba Place Fellowship, Neta serves on the Women's Council and occasionally teaches.

Together they lead one of Reba's five "clusters" of small groups. A recent book they coauthored is *Glimpses of Glory— 30 Years of Community, The Story of Reba Place Fellowship* (Brethren Press, 1987).